D1123204

A STEP-BY-STEP GUIDE TO
GROWING & DISPLAYING
BONSAI

A STEP-BY-STEP GUIDE TO

GROWING & DISPLAYING
BONSAI

Author
Colin Lewis
Photographer
Neil Sutherland

SMITHMARK

© 1993 CLB Publishing. All rights reserved. No part of this publication may be reproduced, stored in a retrieval system, or transmitted in any form or by any means, electronic, mechanical, photocopying, or otherwise, without first obtaining written permission of the copyright owner.

This edition published in 1994 by SMITHMARK Publishers, Inc., 16 East 32nd Street, New York, NY 10016

SMITHMARK books are available for bulk purchase for sales promotion and premium use. For details write or call the manager of special sales, SMITHMARK Publishers, Inc., East 32nd Street, New York, NY 10016; (212) 532-6600

Produced by CLB Publishing, Godalming Business Centre, Woolsack Way, Godalming, Surrey GU7 1XW England

ISBN 0-8317-5162-2

Printed and bound in Singapore by Tien Wah Press

10 9 8 7 6 5 4 3 2

Acknowledgements

I am particularly grateful to my friends Peter Chan, of Herons Nursery, and Ruth Stafford-Jones, for allowing us to photograph trees from their private collections, and Bill Jordan for his advice and the loan of his photographs of pests and diseases. Thanks are also due to China's Bonsai, for the loan of their workshop, to Sally Strugnell for her excellent design, and to Neil Sutherland for his enthusiasm and endless patience behind the camera.

A bonsai is a work of art, whose beauty is entirely dependent upon the skills of its current caretaker. It is therefore important to record who is responsible for the beauty of the specimen bonsai pictured in this book.

Ruth Stafford-Jones: pages: 12, 17, 21, 92, 96, 118
Peter Chan: pages: 4, 14, 34, 36, 39, 40, 46, 52, 54, 79, 86, 91, 98, 109, 111, 112, 115, All the other trees are from my own collection.
'The Fields of Sekiya' on page 8: reproduced courtesy of Bridgeman Art Library

Credits

Design: Sally Strugnell
Edited: David Gibbon
Photographs: Neil Sutherland
Illustrations: Tim Heyward, courtesy of Bernard Thornton Artists
Typesetting: Colin Lewis & Associates
Production Director: Gerald Hughes
Production: Ruth Arthur, Sally Connolly, Neil Randles, Karen Staff, Jonathan Tickner

THE AUTHOR

Colin Lewis admits to having spent much of his childhood in conversation with trees. In 1974, he combined this affection for trees with his formal training as a designer, and began growing bonsai on the window-sill of his London apartment. In 1989, he travelled to Japan to study bonsai, and now regularly teaches and writes for magazines throughout Europe. He has exhibited trees at the Chelsea Flower Show, the National Bonsai Collection and the Annual Bonsai and Suiseki Exhibition in Osaka, Japan.

PHOTOGRAPHER

Neil Sutherland has more than 25 years' experience in a wide range of photographic fields, including still life, portraiture, reportage, natural history, cookery, landscape and travel. His work has been published in countless books and magazines throughout the world.

Half-title page: *Flowering crab apple,* Malus halliana.

Title page: *Trimming a newly-styled cedar,* Cedrus atlantica.

This page: *Japanese Trident maple,* Acer buergerianum.

CONTENTS

1 INTRODUCTION

What is a Bonsai?

The two syllables of the Japanese word *bonsai* literally translate as 'a tree in a pot', but when combined they acquire an altogether grander meaning. A bonsai is a plant which is established in an aesthetically harmonious container, and has been subjected to a number of horticultural and sculptural techniques in order to create a tree-like image. At one end of the spectrum these images are virtually exact replicas of their full-sized cousins. At the other end they can become almost abstract sculptures, inspired by the landscapes of the mind.

A bonsai is not a naturally dwarfed variety, neither is it treated with any special potion to stop it growing larger. Its growth is not restricted by confining the roots in a pot, but by constant clipping and trimming. The size and shape are entirely determined by its keeper whose horticultural and artistic skills also determine its eventual health and aesthetic quality.

How old is a bonsai?

A bonsai does not have to be old to be good. It is quite possible to create a delightful little tree in an afternoon, as you will see later in this book, although until it is established in its pot it is not a true bonsai.

Having said this, bonsai do improve with age. Bark texture, trunk taper, branch structure, fine twigs and so on require time to develop, even with a helping hand. So over the years, with the right care and attention, a good bonsai can become a better bonsai. However, a poorly designed young tree can only become a poorly designed old tree, so it is essential to get the basic form right from the start.

Origins

No-one knows exactly when the first bonsai was grown, but we do know that the ancient Chinese cultivated miniature landscapes in shallow containers. Complete with trees, rocks and mosses, these landscapes, or *penjing*, were the forerunners of bonsai. The first pictorial records of penjing appeared in Chinese temple murals during the Han dynasty, around 200BC.

Single tree plantings came later, but exactly when is unclear. These were called *pun-sai*, the Chinese root of the Japanese word bonsai. In fact the Japanese and Chinese characters for the two terms are identical. When the Chinese invaded Japan in the Middle Ages they introduced, amongst other things, the Buddhist religion. The monks at that time were custodians of all forms of cultural heritage and took with them their written language, their art and their bonsai. For centuries the ownership of bonsai was restricted to those of noble

The Japanese characters for 'bonsai' are identical to the Chinese for 'pun-sai'. Both translate as 'a tree in a pot'.

Above: *The pollarded willow is a familiar sight in northern Europe. This ten-inch high bonsai is pruned back annually, in exactly the same way as its full-sized counterpart.*

Below: *'The classic pine'. An illustration from a Japanese bonsai instruction manual, published in 1829.*

birth or high office. At that time all bonsai were created from ancient stunted trees collected from the mountains, where their constant battle with the harsh environment had restricted their size and given them gnarled and twisted shapes. The tenacity of these trees was held in such reverence that they were deemed to posses spiritual qualities which would be inherited by their owners.

It was not until this century that the ordinary citizen began to practise bonsai, by which time it had become a highly refined and structured discipline. Such was the commitment of the dedicated bonsai artist that a group of them decided to further their art by forming the 'bonsai village', Omiya, which is now an outer suburb of Tokyo and a mecca for bonsai enthusiasts the world over.

Bonsai in the West
The Second World War was responsible for the spread of bonsai to the West. British and American troops returning from the far east brought memories, pictures and some live examples of these curious little trees. Few knew what they were or how to care for them, but in spite of this there are still a few of these original imports alive today.

As the awareness gradually spread, so did the thirst for more knowledge. A few western enthusiasts visited Japan to learn more and returned to spread the word. By the late sixties small commercial nurseries were in business, importing a few hundred trees a year. Nowadays bonsai is a household word and hundreds of thousands of plants are imported annually, although not all from Japan. Many come from China, Korea, Taiwan and Israel. These are tropical species which do not tolerate our climate and must be kept indoors for much of the year. Trees do not grow well under these conditions. They prefer to be exposed to the sun, wind and rain, where their seasonal changes can be fully appreciated.

The future
It is the responsibility of each dedicated bonsai enthusiast to develop the art further by applying the techniques to local species, creating new styles in the process. Therefore, in this book we concentrate entirely on familiar species which will happily thrive outdoors all year round with very little extra winter protection. But there is only so much you can learn from the printed page. Practical experience is the best teacher. If you are really keen you can attend one of the international conventions held each year in many countries. Here, people from all over the world find friendship, peace and harmony through their shared interest in the simple art of cultivating little trees in pots.

Above: A first-day cover, produced in commemoration of the World Bonsai Convention, held in Omiya, Japan in 1989. This indicates the significance of bonsai in modern Japanese culture.

Below: A commercial bonsai 'farm' near Takamatsu, Japan, where field after field of developing bonsai can be seen. These black pines are about twelve years old.

Bonsai: art or horticulture?

At its highest level, bonsai is pure sculpture; living plant material providing the medium while horticulture provides the means by which the artist creates. However, the pleasure each individual gains from growing bonsai will vary according to their reasons for taking up the hobby. For example, a keen gardener may regard bonsai as a new horticultural challenge, as might a plant lover living in a flat with only a balcony for a garden. On the other hand, someone from an artistic background may discover in bonsai the one medium through which they can achieve creative fulfilment.

As a beginner you will probably be more concerned with the horticulture and a little nervous of some of the techniques. But within a short time you will gain confidence as you see your trees respond to the treatment. As confidence grows you will try new ideas. Some of these experiments will succeed but some will inevitably fail. However, from each failure you learn a little more, until you eventually understand what nature will, and will not allow you to do. So regardless of whether you want to grow bonsai as a horticultural or an artistic challenge, the most important thing is that you enjoy your hobby.

Inspirations

We are all surrounded by trees of one sort or another, and these naturally form the basis of all bonsai artists' inspiration. But just looking at trees is not enough – you have to really *see* them in order subconsciously to analyse their structure, so you can reproduce more authentic images in miniature.

Ask an eight-year-old to draw a tree and you will probably be presented with a straight brown trunk topped by a solid green circle. The child will know that the trunk is grey rather than brown, and that a tree has visible branches supporting a crown which will certainly not be round. Even so, children lack the analytical ability necessary to transfer this knowledge onto paper.

Most adults do have this ability, but learning how to use it in the bonsai context can take a little practise. Spend as much time as possible studying trees, single specimens or groups, especially during the winter months when the structures of deciduous varieties are clearly visible. You will notice how the branches on younger trees tend to grow upwards while those on older trees are more horizontal. You can see how all branches grow out towards the nearest available space in the canopy in order to reach the light. Young trees growing close to larger ones will also grow away from their neighbours for much the same reason.

If you look up into the canopy of old pines you will find the branches twist and turn in all directions, reflecting the influence of the weather on the supple young shoots. You will also find natural jins and sharis and will be able to trace how they were formed years ago. You don't have to travel to the wild mountain sides to see these things, they are all around us, in our parks and gardens, and form the basis for many bonsai styles.

But if you do go further afield you will be in for a real treat. Mountain trees grow in thin, poor soil and are exposed to high winds and storms. Their constant battle for survival imparts to them

3 The stylistic representation of trees is deeply entrenched in Japanese art as this early nineteenth century print by Hokusai demonstrates. These black pines, near the Sumida river, are clearly influenced by the traditional literati school (see page 38).

1 The Japanese are almost fanatic about shaping trees. This black pine is growing next to a footpath in Kyoto. Each shoot is individually pruned every two or three years.

2 You don't have to travel far to find inspiration. Notice how the branch structure on this oak, growing in an English suburban garden, echoes that of the Japanese pine on the left.

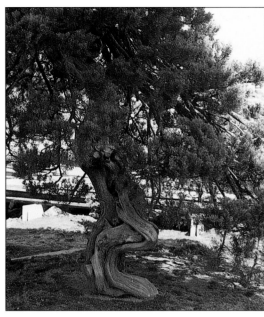

4 *This Chinese Juniper, growing in a Japanese landscape garden, is hundreds of years old. Its heavy, gnarled old trunk displays a wealth of natural sharis and jins.*

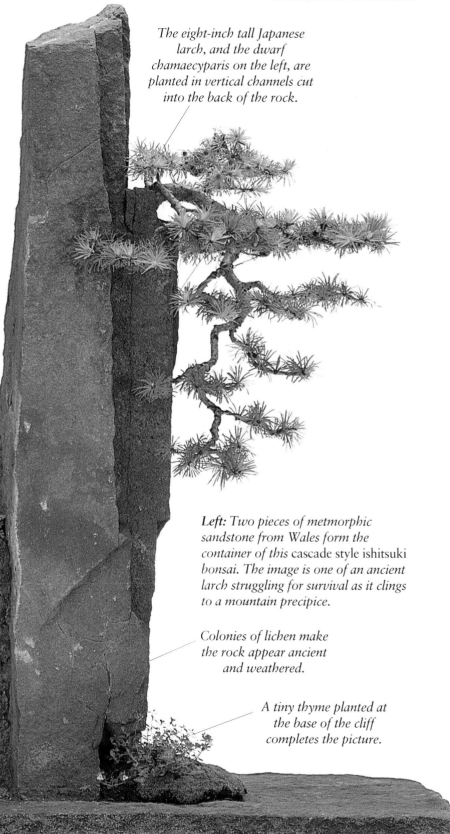

The eight-inch tall Japanese larch, and the dwarf chamaecyparis on the left, are planted in vertical channels cut into the back of the rock.

Left: Two pieces of metmorphic sandstone from Wales form the container of this cascade style ishitsuki bonsai. The image is one of an ancient larch struggling for survival as it clings to a mountain precipice.

Colonies of lichen make the rock appear ancient and weathered.

A tiny thyme planted at the base of the cliff completes the picture.

immense character: twisted and gnarled branches, roots exposed by soil erosion and trunks stripped almost bare of their bark. Here we find the inspiration behind styles like windswept, root-over-rock and literati and cascade.

The importance of photography

Wherever you travel take a camera with you to record what you see. You will soon build up a valuable reference library of photographs which will be a great help when working on difficult new material.

It is also a good idea to create photographic records of your bonsai as they develop over the years. The changes may well be too subtle to notice as you inspect each tree daily, but when you look at pictures taken two or three years ago, the differences can be quite dramatic. To be reminded of how much a tree has developed in just a few years can be very heartening.

Keep your pictures in an album and record the date they were taken. Alongside each picture record other details such as soil used, repotting time, feeding regime, and any other information which may be of interest in the future. You will find yourself referring to these records time and time again, and if you should ever part with the bonsai, its potted history will increase its value to its new owner.

Size and age

One of the first questions people ask on their initial encounter with bonsai is, 'How old is it?' They are naturally fascinated by these ancient-looking specimens, and the thought that they have been cared for by successive generations of devoted artists. In many cases, especially with collected wild trees, it is impossible to know the exact age, one can only guess. As one famous bonsai master says: 'You should never ask a beautiful woman her age'.

Sadly, a few unscrupulous dealers cash in on this fascination with the age of bonsai, and exaggerate the ages of their stock. If the image is one of an eighty-year-old tree, they will claim this to be the true age. Factors such as immature bark texture and unhealed pruning wounds expose their deceit. Such dealers, however, are rare, and tend not to be bonsai specialists.

Once you have grown a few bonsai yourself, you will realise just how unimportant the true age really is compared with the apparent age. More significant is the length of time the tree has been in training as a bonsai. Even this is of secondary importance when compared to the beauty of form, colour and texture.

Size is another factor whose importance is frequently over-rated. It is often assumed that the larger the bonsai, the older, and therefore the better it is. This is not true. It is also often assumed that bigger bonsai are technically and aesthetically more difficult to create and maintain. Also not true.

In fact a small or *shohin* bonsai requires more ingenuity and patience to create, because the artist has to work with fewer elements, yet still has to aspire to the same aesthetic standards which apply to larger trees.

A shohin bonsai also demands far more constant attention to maintain. The pots dry out quicker, shoots outgrow the design more often and, if left to grow for too long, will sap the energy from the fine twigs, causing them to wither and die.

To demonstrate this principle we have selected three established bonsai of identical species (English elm, *Ulmus procera*). They are similar in style and all originated from suckers which invaded my allotment. However, they are all very different in size, and are shown here in proportion to each other. What's more, they took very different lengths of time to develop.

This tiny shohin is only six-and-a-half inches tall from the rim of the pot. It started its bonsai career as a tiny shoot bearing only five leaves, and has been in training for a total of eighteen years. The surface roots and trunk formation are excellent, and the branch structure, which is the result of many years of constant pinching and detailed fine wiring, compares favourably with any of the finest large bonsai.

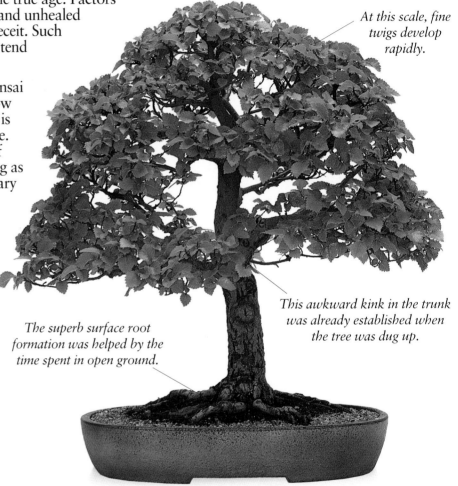

At this scale, fine twigs develop rapidly.

This awkward kink in the trunk was already established when the tree was dug up.

The superb surface root formation was helped by the time spent in open ground.

This medium-size bonsai stands eleven inches tall from the rim of the pot. It was collected eleven years ago and spent the next two years in the flower border, where it received some initial training. The larger pot has helped to speed up its development.

At this scale the foliage remains coarse, even though the tree was leaf-pruned a month before this photograph was taken (see page 60).

Young shoots are still being allowed to develop into mature branches.

The one-sided root formation is typical of collected suckers at this size. It is too well established to change at this stage.

At twenty-two inches tall, this bonsai is quite large, although by no means the largest I have seen. It was collected only six years ago from a roadside verge, and was planted directly into a bonsai container. Originally, the tree was seven feet tall, and was reduced on collection, using the technique outlined on page 32.

2

HOW A BONSAI GROWS

Root to leaf

Your bonsai is the result of an interaction between you and nature, and the success of everything you do relies upon the tree's natural response to your actions. In order to get the best out of your hobby it is important to have at least a basic understanding of how a tree works.

Roots

Roots have three functions. One, quite simply, is to hold the tree steady in the soil. This is performed by thick, strong roots which radiate from the base of the trunk. Evidence which came to light after the great storm in 1987 in the UK suggests that these roots only penetrate the soil a few feet, and the existence of an extensive tap root was only a myth.

The second function is to store nutrients during the dormant period, ready for use when growth resumes in spring.

The third function is to absorb water and nutrients, via tiny, single-cell protrusions called root hairs, which clothe the young roots as they grow.

Root problems

Apart from insect attack the only serious problem you will need to cope with is root rot, which is easier to prevent than cure. Decay is caused by microscopic fungi or bacteria which take hold on dead roots, so the simple answer is to ensure that the roots remain healthy at all times.

The first precaution is to use a free-draining soil with plenty of air spaces. This prevents the roots 'drowning' and is inhospitable to unwanted fungi. Similarly, you should never allow the soil to dry out, as this will also kill young, tender roots, exposing them to decay.

The second precaution is to avoid over-feeding. Roots absorb water by osmosis, whereby a weak solution passes through a membrane (the wall of the root) towards a stronger solution. If the water in the soil contains a stronger solution of nutrients than that in the root, water will pass from the root back into the soil, damaging the roots and depriving the tree of water.

The first signs of root rot are yellowing or wilting of the leaves, die-back of young shoots, or a sudden lack of vigour. Your first reaction is likely to be to increase the feed and water, either of which will compound the problem. The best course of action is to follow the instructions for emergency repotting on page 49.

The trunk and branches

Like roots, the trunk and branches also perform three functions. The first is structural, supporting the branches and foliage.

Sapwood or xylem
Cambium
Phloem
Bark
Heartwood

1 *This cross-section shows the different layers that make up the trunk. The heartwood is essentially dead and acts in a structural capacity.*

This gorgeous azalea (Rhododendron indicum 'Eikan') is kept in vibrant health by its owner, Ruth Stafford-Jones. The bi-coloured flowers are what makes this variety so desirable.

The second, also like roots, is to store nutrients until needed. This is done in specially adapted cells which radiate from the centre of the trunk in bundles called medullary rays.

The third function is to carry water and nutrients from one part of the tree to another. This takes place towards the outer edge of the trunk, either side of the cambium layer.

The cambium layer

This is really the 'magic' part of the tree, responsible for controlling the growth. It is a single-cell layer just beneath the bark and appears green when the bark is scraped away in most species (in some conifers it is orange or yellow).

2 *The growing tip of a root, showing the single-cell root hairs and the main transport vessels.*

Root hairs

During the growing season the cambium layer produces a new layer of tissue on either side. On the inside is the sapwood, or xylem, through which the water is transported from the roots throughout the tree. Each season this xylem is replaced by a new layer, creating the familiar growth rings.

On the outside the new layer is called the phloem, and this is responsible for distributing the sugars produced in the leaves to other parts of the tree. This, too, is replaced each year and the build-up of old phloem layers forms the thick, corky bark we see on older trees.

The cambium layer is also responsible for producing new roots in cuttings and air layers, and adventitious buds, as well as the tissue which heals over wounds. When grafting, the cambium layers of the two components fuse together, enabling them to operate as one plant.

Foliage

All leaves are basically food factories, using light as a catalyst to convert water supplied by the roots and carbon dioxide absorbed from the air into sugars, in a process called photosyntheses. These sugars provide growth energy to the plant.

During the day the leaves 'breathe in' through small pores called stomata, and at night they expel the excess oxygen and other gaseous by-products. They also allow water to evaporate through the surface in order to keep up a constant flow.

Some leaves, particularly the needles of pines and spruces, have a waxy coating to help conserve moisture during the winter, when the roots are frozen and unable to function. This coating also serves to prevent snow and ice adhering to the surfaces and suffocating the tree.

Species such as the eucalypts have a similar coating to prevent too much transpiration of water in hot, dry weather, while other leaves have fine hairs which achieve the same result by reducing the air flow over the surface.

Species such as Japanese maples, which prefer dappled shade, have a very thin skin, or cuticle, which scorches easily when exposed to hot sun.

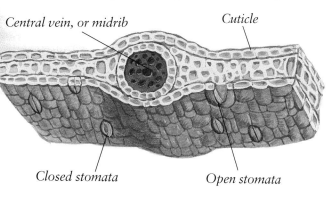

Central vein, or midrib   *Cuticle*

Closed stomata   *Open stomata*

3 *Right: Cross-section of a leaf from a broadleaved tree. Each leaf is a tiny 'food factory', providing nourishment for the plant during the summer months.*

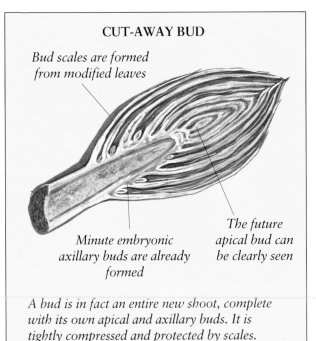

1 *Delicate elm buds unfurl to reveal minute, bright green leaves.*

How buds work

Buds come in many different shapes and sizes, but they all have one thing in common. They all contain an entire new shoot, minutely formed and tightly packed within a protective sheath of scales.

To get an idea of what a bud looks like inside just cut a savoy cabbage in half. You will clearly see the foreshortened shoot and folded leaves, with the dark outer leaves serving as scales. It is hard to imagine how so much could be contained in a bud which may be no bigger than a pinhead.

• Terminal or apical buds are formed at the tips of the current year's shoots and are usually the largest since they contain next year's extension growth. These are often flanked by smaller axillary buds.

• Axillary buds are formed along the length of the shoot, in each leaf axil (the point where the leaf stem, or petiole, joins the shoot), or in the axils of the bud scales. They will either produce the shorter side shoots next year or remain dormant.

• Dormant buds are generally axillary buds which failed to open in the year following their formation. They can remain, barely visible, for several years until they are stimulated into growth by pruning, feeding or increased light levels.

• Adventitious buds can emerge anywhere on old wood, around pruning cuts or even on roots. They are the tree's response to improved conditions or its method of regeneration after loss of foliage mass. Adventitious buds tend to produce vigorous, sappy shoots.

CUT-AWAY BUD

Bud scales are formed from modified leaves

Minute embryonic axillary buds are already formed

The future apical bud can be clearly seen

A bud is in fact an entire new shoot, complete with its own apical and axillary buds. It is tightly compressed and protected by scales.

1 *Spruce (illustrated) and needle-leaved junipers produce masses of buds. They open quickly, exposing tight clusters of needles, which rapidly extend into soft, tender shoots.*

Above: *With Japanese red maples, the colour in spring is every bit as impressive as it is in autumn. The leaves are smaller, and much brighter.*

Apical bud.

Axillary buds.

The apical buds on lateral shoots are less well developed.

Apical bud.

Dormant buds lurk around the base of every developed bud.

Adventitious buds develop readily around the cessation scars.

Above: *In winter, many trees can be identified by their buds. However, all deciduous shoots bear apical and axillary buds, as well as showing 'cessation scars', indicating the points at which one year's growth ended and the next one began, where dormant buds occur.*

3 The scales on maple buds peel back so the brightly coloured leaves develop. At this stage they are very prone to frost and aphid damage.

4 Pine buds don't open in the same way as other trees. They elongate, shedding the papery scales as they do so. The needles elongate and peel away from the shoot as it develops.

5 These fat, prominent buds at the tips of azalea shoots are in fact flower buds. The growth buds are nestled in the axils of the leaves just below them.

2 Larch buds lose their papery scales to expose tiny 'shaving brushes' of new needles. Larch shoots emerge suddenly from the centres of these clusters, retaining the mass of needles at the base, providing plenty of dormant buds. If the buds are dislodged at this stage they cannot form dormant buds around the base, so treat with care.

19

3

THE RAW MATERIAL

Buying bonsai

Many newcomers to bonsai begin by being tempted to buy one at a garden centre. The so-called bonsai offered for sale at garden centres are invariably tropical species from the Far or Middle-East. They may have been in stock for some time and be suffering from neglect. Tropical species cannot tolerate our climate, so they must be kept inside for most of the year. This is fine if you can provide a controlled environment, which is not easy. If you are intent on growing bonsai indoors, go to a reputable specialist nursery, whose plants will be well cared for and whose staff will be able to offer good advice.

The same advice applies to buying hardy species. Specialist growers know their stuff, so benefit from their experience by asking as many questions as you can. Bonsai people are always glad to help. Meanwhile, the following points will help you get the best value.

Price
• Bonsai are expensive because it takes time to create them by hand, and they are transportedhalf way round the world. Less than a reasonable price will only buy a 'half finished' bonsai, requiring several years' work to refine.

Health
• It is best to buy any plant during the growing season so you can be sure it is alive and healthy. If you buy in winter scratch the bark a little: if it is green underneath the plant is alive, if not, it is dead.

• Avoid plants with die back, damaged leaves etc., which may be symptoms of disease.

• Check the tree is firm in its pot. Hold the trunk and *gently* try to rock it from side to side. If it moves put it back on the shelf.

• Check the soil. This should be loose and porous, moist but not waterlogged. The pot must have adequate drainage holes, which are not blocked. There should be no established weeds in the pot. Liverwort and pearlwort are both signs of poor soil.

Appearance
• The surface roots should look natural as they emerge from the trunk. The trunk should have a natural shape and taper, with no unsightly scars or graft unions. Avoid bonsai with exaggerated spirals and hairpin bends.

• The branches should be evenly distributed around the trunk, the lower ones being thicker than those at the top.

• Make sure there are no wire marks on the trunk or branches or, worse still, that there is no wire embedded in the bark.

Aftercare
• Always ask the nurseryman about the tree's specific horticultural requirements such as watering, feeding, winter protection and so on, and try to find out when it was last repotted so you know when next to tackle this task.

WHAT NOT TO LOOK FOR!
Neither of these plants could be called a bonsai.

The pine (above) is a three-year-old seedling which was pruned once at the end of its second year. The grower wired the trunk to make it look authentic, without altering the shape. Its only potential for bonsai is as raw material, needing to be grown in the ground for many years. The plastic pot reveals the nursery's desire for a fast buck.

The little Japanese maple (right) is four years old. Its trunk has been shaped with wire by somebody who has clearly never seen a real tree! There is no way this freak could be turned into a bonsai. The only hope would be to cut the trunk below the first bend and start again.

Japanese cypress (Cryptomeria Japonica). *This maginificent bonsai is very ancient indeed, well over a hundred years old. Its trunk is hollow all the way up and the branches are by now very brittle.*

Above: *When you see trees presented like this you can be fairly confident you are getting good value. They are all healthy and weed-free, and the fertiliser pellets on each pot show they are well cared for.*

Garden centre stock

The real essence of bonsai is creating your own, and the most readily available raw material is to be found in garden centres. There is a bewildering range of species and sizes to choose from, which only serves to make the decision more difficult. The following points will help you to make a sensible choice and avoid wasting your money on inappropriate plants.

What species?
• Deciduous or conifer? It doesn't really matter, but bear in mind that, while conifers make more 'instant' bonsai and deciduous species take longer to develop, the latter will reward you with changes in colour and form as the seasons change.

• It may sound odd, but avoid slow growing or dwarf varieties because they can take a long time to respond to training. The main exceptions to this rule are dwarf spruces which, ironically, make superb bonsai.

• If you want a flowering species choose one which flowers on the previous year's wood. If the blooms are borne on current year's growth the shoots will need to grow disproportionately long before flowering begins.

• Test the branches to check that they are supple enough to be shaped by wiring.

• Finally, decide on a variety which already has smallish leaves or needles and shows a readiness to produce buds on older wood.

Final choice
Once you decide on the species, you need to select the plant with the most potential.

• Examine each plant carefully, starting at the base. Expose the surface roots to see if they appear natural.

• There should be plenty of low branches which still bear foliage close to the trunk. This will present you with many possibilities when you get home and begin to design your bonsai.

• Don't assume that the existing trunk line will necessarily be the final one, or that the new bonsai will be the same size as the raw material. These options should be carefully considered at your leisure, when you will have time to find the tree's hidden 'soul'.

• Finally, carry out all the health checks outlined in 'Buying bonsai' on page 20.

This little azalea was chosen for its superb root spread. It took only three years to reach this stage, and rewards me with a mass of crimson flowers each May.

1 At first you may be tempted by 'unusual' trunk shapes like this. But in the case of this plant, unusual means unnatural and it would never make a good bonsai.

2 Many garden centre plants are grafted onto sturdier root stocks, causing an unsightly swelling which gets worse as the tree ages. These should be avoided.

SUITABLE GARDEN CENTRE SPECIES
Some of the most reliable species which have a proven record of suitability.

Acer – *palmatum,*
Japonicum, (maples)
Azalea (botanically
Rhododendron)
Berberis
Betula (birches)
Buxus (box)
Carpinus (hornbeam)
Cedrus (cedar –
brevifolia is best)
Chaenomeles (quince)

Chamaecyparis (dwarf
varieties are best)
Cotoneaster
Crataegus (hawthorn)
Cryptomeria
Fagus (beech)
Juniperus (all types)
Larix (larches)
Ligustrum (privet)
Lonicera nitida (hedge
honeysuckle)

Picea (spruces)
Pinus (pines)
Potentilla
Prunus (flowering
cherries)
Pyracantha
Spirea
Taxus (yew)
Ulmus (elms)
Wisteria
Zelkova

4 *At first sight this dwarf cotoneaster seems ideal for bonsai. Closer inspection reveals that all the branches emerge straight from the soil and there is no trunk, making it useless.*

3 *The odd weed shows that the plant has become established in the pot, but growth like this liverwort indicates poor drainage and unhealthy roots.*

5 *Good surface roots are essential in bonsai. Don't be tempted by bizarre root formations like this, they may seem interesting at first but ultimately you will regret the purchase.*

Propagation from seed

If you have the patience there is nothing more rewarding than growing bonsai from seed, regardless of whether you intend to train it from scratch or grow the plant on to form larger raw material. Sowing seed for bonsai is carried out in the same way as for other purposes and is familiar to most people, but the process is outlined here for the complete novice. Extra care is needed when pricking out seedlings.

Here are a few tips.

• Before buying your seeds make sure the species is suitable (*see page 23*). Look in the classified ads in gardening magazines for seed merchants.

• Use a sandier than normal soil with no added fertiliser.

• Seeds with hard cases will germinate quicker if the shell is cracked or slit.

• The seeds of most hardy species need to be stratified before they will germinate. This involves exposing them to periods of low temperature, as they would naturally experience in winter. The best plan is to leave such seeds outside, but if you want to germinate them indoors you can simulate winter by mixing the seeds with dry-ish sand and placing them in the salad compartment of a refrigerator for a few weeks. I have known field maple seeds to germinate within two weeks, while still in the refrigerator.

• If you germinate your seeds indoors, harden them off gradually before siting them permanently outside.

• The seeds of some species, for example hornbeam and hawthorn, may take two years to germinate, so be patient.

1 Having cleaned your seeds, space them out evenly on a layer of fine compost in a seed tray. Hard seeds germinate better if the shells are chipped with a sharp knife.

2 Cover the seeds with a layer of compost, to a depth of roughly the thickness of the seeds. Don't press this down, leave it loose so the seeds can breathe.

3 The seed tray should be watered with a spray. Including a copper-based fungicide such as Cheshunt compound helps prevent decay as well as 'damping off' of the new seedlings.

4 Cover the seed tray, leaving the ventilation holes fully open. Place the tray outside, where the seeds will be subjected to the natural seasonal changes in temperature.

5 Once the seedlings have their first true leaves, gently tease them out. Hold the leaves, not the stem.

6 Use a sharp, sterile blade to cut through the tap root, leaving enough side roots to sustain the seedling.

7 When planting the seedlings in their growing pots, spread the roots radially from the stem. This is the first, essential step in bonsai training, ensuring a good root formation for the future.

Even after many generations, the importance of spreading the seedling's roots is clear.

This massive, informal upright Japanese maple, owned by Ruth Stafford-Jones, is one of the finest trees ever to leave Japan. It is curious to think that it, too, was once a tiny seedling.

8 Cover the roots with bonsai soil. Don't press the soil down as this may damage the tender young roots. Water gently and place the seedlings in a sheltered spot until new growth appears.

Cuttings

The advantage of propagating from cuttings of any type is that you can reproduce the exact characteristics of the parent plant, whereas plants grown from seed may vary.

There are three types of cutting appropriate for bonsai: softwood, hardwood and root cuttings.

Softwood cuttings use new growth as the name implies. These should be taken in early summer, and need to be kept in an enclosed, humid atmosphere until they have taken root.

Hardwood cuttings use mature growth and are taken in the autumn, usually using shoots which have grown that year, although some species will root from wood two or more years old.

Root cuttings are suitable for species which naturally throw up shoots, or suckers, from the roots. They can be taken any time between November and April, using roots up to three inches thick.

This little Cornish elm started as a root cutting nine years ago. The trunk was later hollowed out to give a really ancient appearance.

1 Softwood cuttings are taken in May and June. The lower leaves and the growing tips are cut off using a very sharp blade.

2 Handle the cuttings carefully, and insert them into sandy compost to a depth equal to about a third of their length. It is not necessary to use hormone treatment, although spraying them with systemic fungicide will help prevent decay, thus improving results.

3 Commercial propagators are ideal. They have clear covers with controlled ventilation. Make your own by placing a plastic bag over a pot. Spray cuttings daily until new growth appears.

CHINESE JUNIPER CUTTINGS

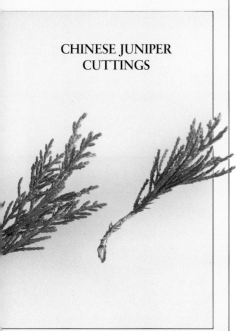

Chinese junipers root very easily, although they can take up to a year. Take three-inch shoots of last year's growth in June and prepare them as shown.

4 *There are two types of hardwood cuttings: nodal, and heel cuttings. Nodal cuttings should be cut cleanly with a sharp knife, just below a leaf node, or axillary bud, as shown.*

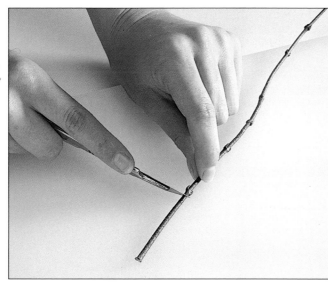

5 *When taking heel cuttings, pull the shoot away from its parent, retaining a sliver of bark, or heel. Trim the heel with a sharp knife.*

6 *Plant the cuttings to a depth of at least half their length, either in open ground or in a deep pot. Make the holes with a dibber to avoid damaging the ends of the cuttings.*

7 *When trimming root cuttings use a very sharp blade as their soft bark crushes easily. Leaving a few feeder roots will help the cutting on its way.*

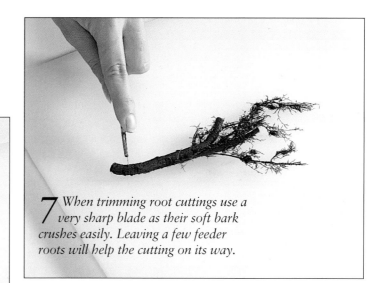

8 *For single-tree styles the root cutting should be planted vertically, making sure it is the right way up!*

9 *For clump or raft styles, the root cuttings should be planted on their sides. A large number of new shoots will be produced.*

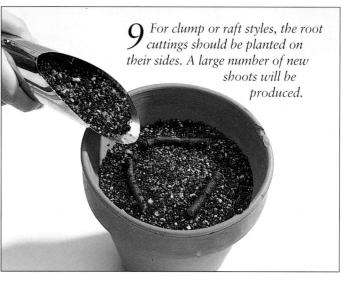

Air layers

Most gardens will have a few shrubs or a hedge which has been regularly clipped over the years. This naturally produces areas where there are many small and interestingly-shaped branches bearing a network of small twigs. It takes little imagination to see how good some of these would look in pots after a little training – if only they had roots! If you're lucky you might have a flowering cherry, quince or pyracantha.

Spruce, cypresses, yew and junipers all work well, although pines don't co-operate. Most deciduous species will layer successfully but some take longer than others.

Air layering is a technique which enables you to induce roots to emerge exactly at the point you want them. It is like taking a cutting without actually severing the branch from its parent plant until the roots have grown. You can even carry out a certain amount of pruning and wire training beforehand.

This technique also comes in useful when you have an 'ex-bonsai' which has become so overgrown that it needs to be cut right back and have new branches grown on from scratch. By air layering the old branches you can use them to create more bonsai.

The best time to tackle this technique is early to mid summer, as soon as the leaves have fully hardened. It is a good idea to give the tree a dose of fertiliser high in phosphates before you start to get it in the mood for making roots and remember never to let the polythene-covered moss dry out.

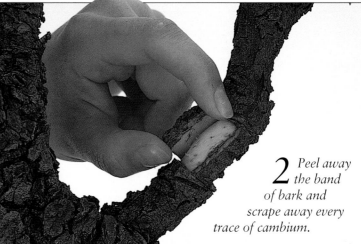

1 Make two cuts round the trunk, and another one vertically. Cut right through to the wood.

2 Peel away the band of bark and scrape away every trace of cambium.

Above: These radial roots are typical of the kind of structure which can be achieved by air layering. The trick is to layer early in the year to give the new roots time to establish before winter.

3 Take a strip of clear polythene, about nine inches long and six inches wide, and tie it fairly tightly an inch below the wound. Leave an overlap of an inch and a half.

4 *Fill the polythene with fresh, moist sphagnum moss – the type sold by florists for hanging baskets – then tie the polythene loosly at the top. Keep the moss moist and inspect frequently until new roots are visible.*

5 *Once the new roots have begun to turn brown the branch can be severed below the polythene.*

6 *Gently peel away the plastic. Take care not to damage the very delicate roots. If you allow the moss to fall away it will tear the roots.*

7 *Place the undisturbed root ball, complete with moss, in a deep pot filled with fresh bonsai soil. Don't press down on the tender roots.*

8 *Trim all long shoots to reduce demand on the new roots and put the new tree in a sheltered spot for a few weeks. Spray daily and feed well after the first month.*

Growing your own

Two of the most desirable features in any bonsai are mature bark and pronounced taper of the trunk. These properties are always difficult, and often impossible, to achieve when a tree has spent all its life growing slowly in the confines of a shallow bonsai pot.

Traditionally, the most revered specimens were created from stunted plants collected from the mountains of Japan. But nowadays, to do this would be highly irresponsible almost anywhere in the world and certainly illegal in most western countries.

The only satisfactory solution is to grow your own raw material in a way which produces all the desirable characteristics in as short a time as possible. To do this you need to encourage the lower branches to grow in order to thicken the lower part of the trunk. If the base of the trunk is mulched with straw or leaf mould the bark will swell and crack, making it look even older.

The result is a heavy trunk with considerable taper, flaky bark and many old scars – all the characteristics of great age.

This technique of growing raw material is ideal for most deciduous species, but not suitable for conifers since they will not regenerate growth once all the foliage-bearing branches have been removed.

When growing conifers in open ground prune back as hard as you can every two years, while still leaving some foliage on each branch. Each spring pinch out about half of every new 'candle' as soon as they are big enough to handle. This will produce masses of branches and shoots to choose from when you eventually come to style the tree.

The example we have chosen is a Siberian elm which is nine years old and has spent all its life in open ground. Each year it was heavily fed to encourage rapid growth. The top branches were kept trimmed back during each growing season while the lower ones were allowed to grow unchecked for two years at a time. Every two years all branches were removed completely and the whole process repeated.

The drastic root pruning shown here is successful with most elms and trident maple. With other species it is advisable to reduce the roots in stages during successive springs, repotting into a smaller container each time.

This elm will be placed in a sheltered position for a few weeks, until new growth appears. It will be fed heavily throughout the next season, so that in a year's time it will be ready for initial styling (see page 72).

1 In full leaf this Siberian elm was just a bush, but in winter the trunk's potential can clearly be seen. Once dug, all the soil should be washed away from the roots with a hose.

2 Every branch and shoot is cut off, leaving just the basic trunk. Prune the top branches selectively so you leave as uniform a taper as possible.

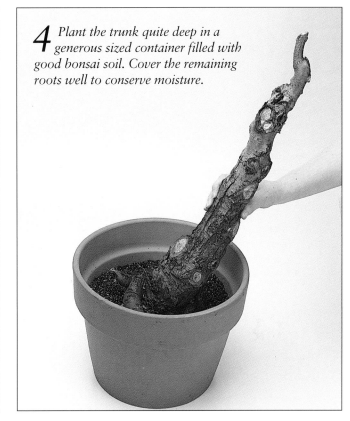

4 Plant the trunk quite deep in a generous sized container filled with good bonsai soil. Cover the remaining roots well to conserve moisture.

Azaleas grow very slowly. A trunk like this can take a very long time to form.

This massive azalea has been grown in open ground since 1952. It has been growing in a container for three years and is already taking shape nicely.

3 Cut the roots as far back as you can, while leaving a few finer roots to sustain the plant until it can grow more. Use a sharp saw as the roots are fibrous and easily tear.

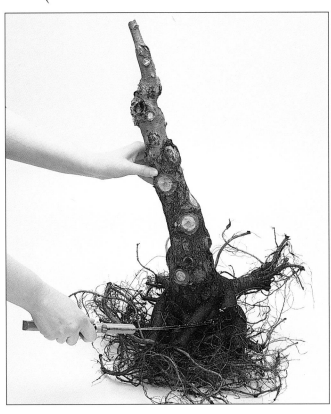

5 The tree should be placed in a polytunnel until new growth is established. This can take time and may not appear until mid-summer or beyond.

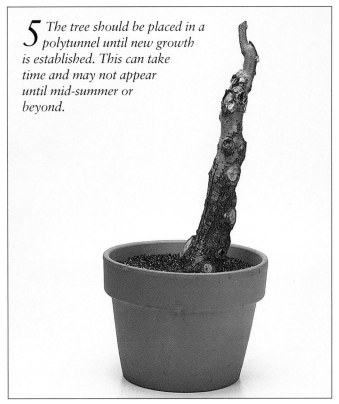

Reducing taller trees

Some people prefer to grow very large bonsai but are unable to find suitable raw material growing in open ground, and are unwilling to spend the required number of years to grow their own. The only alternative is to acquire a suitable plant from a tree nursery. These trees are intended for planting in parks, streets or large gardens and are grown in the ground for a number of years before being established in containers prior to sale.

When seeking out such material make sure it is well established in its container; moss and weeds growing in the soil is a good indication of this. Examine the surface roots to ensure they are evenly distributed. Scratch away a sliver of bark on each one – if it appears green beneath the bark the root is alive, if it appears brown or grey the root is dead.

Cutting off the top section of the trunk will force a tree to throw out shoots from the remaining trunk, but their location cannot be predicted and there is every chance that they will be limited to the area immediately around the cut. This is useless for bonsai purposes unless you intend to grow a broom-style zelkova *(see page 82)*. So you will need to counter this by selecting a plant which has a good number of low branches.

You can carry out this initial pruning any time between November and the following June, but the ideal time is in early spring, just before the buds break.

Leave the tree in its original container for at least a year before attempting to plant it in a bonsai pot. During this time you can begin to style it by wiring and pruning.

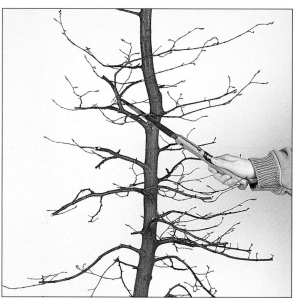

2 *Choose a branch for the new leader and make the cut diagonally downwards from this, towards a lower branch on the opposite side of the trunk.*

3 *Use typewriter correction fluid, or white paint, to mark a natural flowing trunk line from the new leader to the top branch.*

1 *This twelve feet tall hornbeam (Carpinus betulus) was bought from a landscape tree nursery, and was chosen because it had plenty of low branches.*

4 *Carve the wound gradually up to the line, without tearing the bark. Hollowing out the heartwood a little will help the wound to heal flat, resulting in an almost invisible scar.*

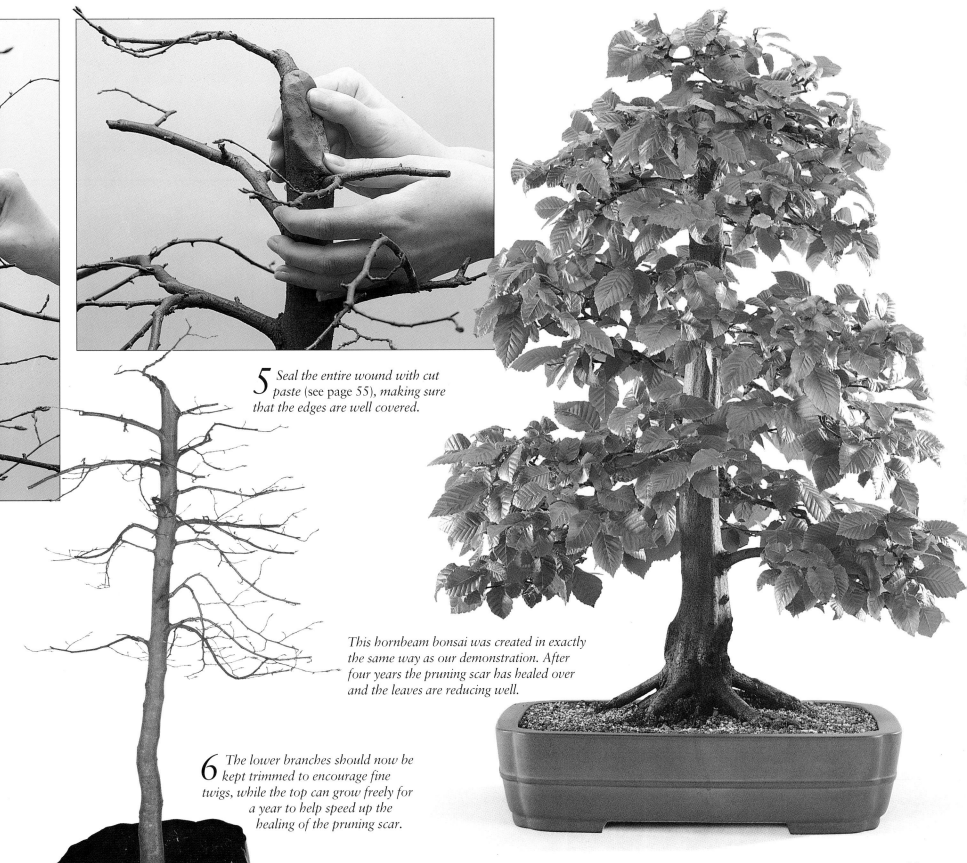

5 Seal the entire wound with cut paste (see page 55), making sure that the edges are well covered.

This hornbeam bonsai was created in exactly the same way as our demonstration. After four years the pruning scar has healed over and the leaves are reducing well.

6 The lower branches should now be kept trimmed to encourage fine twigs, while the top can grow freely for a year to help speed up the healing of the pruning scar.

33

4 HARDWARE
Tools and wire

Tools

All you really need in the way of equipment for your first attempts at growing bonsai are those which you probably already have.

• A pair of sharp scissors • Wire cutters • Secateurs (the bypass type, *not* the anvil variety) • Nail scissors for fine work • A pointed steel hook for combing out roots. (I still use the one I made sixteen years ago).

These tools will do the job almost as well as the specialist Japanese tools shown here. But as you gain experience you will begin to find them a little clumsy at best and totally inadequate at worst. Sooner or later you will want to invest in your first proper bonsai tools, but rather than spend a lot of money on a full set, buy them one or two at a time.

Because they are the cheapest tools you will probably decide to buy a couple of pairs of scissors first, long ones for trimming and short shears for heavier work such as root pruning. This is a good choice and you will soon discover how easy the Japanese tools are to use.

Next you should go for some side cutters which can cut branches cleanly and accurately, and some long-handled wire cutters, designed to cut right up to the tip. The big advantage of both these tools is that they are able to reach the most inaccessible parts of the tree.

Curved branch cutters should come next. These are used for pruning close to the trunk, where a slight hollow is required to help the wound heal over quickly. Some bonsai pliers would be a good idea too. The shape of the jaws makes them ideal for stripping jins and sharis, as well as for manipulating the wire once it has been applied to the tree.

All the other tools are more specialist in their application and can be bought as and when the need arises.

One special note. Always keep your tools sharp by honing them on a fine, oiled sharpening stone, and sterilise them after use by immersing them in methylated spirit.

Wire

Here we show a variety of types and thicknesses of wire. Your first choice may be influenced by economy and availability. Copper wire can be stripped from offcuts of electrical cable, and green, plastic-covered steel wire is readily available at garden centres.

However, once you have tried the custom-made product you will never want to use anything else. The wide variety of gauges, its subdued colour and ease of manipulation make it a joy to work with, in spite of the extra expense. A full explanation of the advantages and disadvantages of the various types of wire appears on page 50.

5mm aluminium bonsai wire is quite strong, and is useful for trunks and heavy branches.

3mm aluminium wire is good for most branches.

1.5mm aluminium bonsai wire, soft, gentle and easy to apply.

Below: *The range of wire I find most useful. I only use the green, plastic-coated wire for anchoring the tree in its pot and for fashioning hooks and ties etc. I get through a lot of wire, and it can be expensive if bought in small quantities. Once you know the thicknesses you use most, it is worth investing in some larger rolls.*

Sturdy shears for cutting roots.

Spring-handled 'snippers' for leaf and fine shoot pruning.

2mm aluminium wire is ideal for wiring young shoots.

Concave cutters for removing branch stubs and hollowing wounds.

Bonsai pliers.

Side cutters for branch removal.

2mm plastic-covered wire is heavy and unwieldy.

Long tweezers have a wide variety of uses in bonsai.

Japanese wire cutters cut right to the tip.

Copper wire stripped from electrical cable.

1mm plastic-coated steel wire.

Long-handled scissors for shoot trimming.

For really fine work, telephone wire or fuse wire is ideal.

Above: *A set of basic Japanese bonsai tools. These can be expensive, but are much easier to use than western tools, and are well worth the investment if you intent to take the hobby seriously.*

Soils

Most plants will survive for limited periods in almost any growing medium – clay, sand, even pure water – but in order to thrive they need rather more. Since bonsai are grown in shallow containers for many years their requirements are quite specific. But before we discuss soil recipes let's consider the various functions of soil.

- The soil's most obvious function is to retain enough moisture and nutrients to ensure a steady supply to the roots between waterings.
- The soil must protect the roots from decay by allowing the free drainage of excess water.
- It must also contain air spaces so the roots can breathe.
- Finally, the soil anchors the tree in its pot, so it should not be too light.

Soil recipes

The standard bonsai soil recipe, which has been tried and tested for many years, contains just two ingredients which, when sifted and mixed in roughly equal proportions, satisfy these four basic requirements.

NOTE: all soil ingredients must be well sifted to remove all the coarse lumps and, more importantly, all the fine particles. Ideally you should be left with particles ranging in size between 2 and 4mm. Any particles finer than this may be difficult to wet once they dry out. They will also clog the soil, impeding drainage and eliminating air spaces. To sift ingredients efficiently make sure they are fairly dry.

Crushed volcanic lava.

Basic mix – 50:50 grit and peat.

More bonsai accessories: soil scoops, plastic mesh for covering drainage holes, a sturdy clamp for bending heavy branches, 'Kyonal' wound sealant and a rice haulm brush.

Organic matter

Organic matter satisfies the first of the four requirements mentioned above. This can be moss peat (as opposed to sedge peat), well-rotted leaf mould, composted forest bark or any of the peat substitutes which are becoming increasingly common.

Don't use any farmyard manure or garden compost, however well rotted, as you will risk introducing all manner of soil-borne diseases.

If you collect your own leaf mould remove any unrotted material which will use up nitrogen from the fertiliser as it continues to decay. Also remove any insects or grubs that you may find. Some people sterilise leaf mould by placing it in a microwave oven for a few minutes. Oak, beech, chestnut and pine leaves produce the best texture.

Grit

Grit, or sifted sharp sand, keeps the soil structure open and adds weight, thus satisfying the remaining three requirements.

It can be quite difficult to find suitable grit, and many people resort to buying horticultural sharp sand and sifting out unsuitably-sized particles. This is extremely laborious, time consuming and wasteful – only about twenty percent of the original volume is useful. Builders

Japanese 'Akadama' clay.

Calcined (baked) clay.

sharp sand should never be used as it often contains impurities which can be harmful to plants.

Flint grit, as used for alpine composts, is good but it has sharp edges which can damage the roots if used carelessly. So be gentle when repotting and don't use too much pressure.

By far the best type I have tried is granite grit. The surface of each particle is uneven, but the edges are not sharp. Grit from fast-flowing streams is also good. Whatever kind of grit you use is not terribly important, however, so long as it is included.

Additives
Soil conditioners
An increasing number of soil conditioners are available to the amateur gardener, ranging from volcanic lava to calcined (baked) clay. The main advantage of using such additives is that they perform the same functions as both organic matter and grit. That is to say they drain well but also retain moisture. Some growers use calcined clay instead of organic matter, and others find trees grown in pure lava do exceptionally well. It is always worth experimenting.

Japanese Clay
Many bonsai nurseries now sell imported Japanese *Akadama* clay, which is specifically produced for bonsai. It retains its granular structure when wet, drains freely, retains moisture and air and allows the roots to grow through the particles. It sounds ideal, and indeed is in Japan, where the climate is predictable. But in our climate you may need to water your trees more often in summer, and keep them out of excessive rain during autumn and winter. However, it is worth trying.

Fertilisers
If you feed your bonsai properly it is not necessary to add fertiliser to the soil, but it does no harm to include a little bonemeal or fish, blood and bone. Add some trace element compound as a matter of course, since none of the ingredients can provide their own.

Sifted peat, note the particle size.

Flint grit (left) and crushed granite.

Above: All bonsai enthusiasts have their own pet soil recipes, some better than others. The ingredients above have all been tried and tested over the years and have been found to be the best. You will see that loam, or garden soil has not been included. This is for a very good reason. Garden soil not only contains all the soil-borne diseases, but it also quickly compacts when watered, forming a dense, soggy mass. Garden compost, farmyard manure and spent mushroom compost are also risky as they can import many unwanted pests and diseases too.

VARIATIONS

Pines
Pines prefer a greater proportion of grit in the soil – up to eighty percent – and the tree's performance will be greatly enhanced if you can include pine needle mould in the mix. There is a naturally-occurring fungus associated with pines which covers the roots in a sheath known as a mycorrhiza. This breaks down the nutrients in the soil into a form which is more readily available to the tree in exchange for a share of the tree's manufactured food supply. It appears as fine white filaments called mycelium, which can be found just below the surface of pine litter.

Flowering and fruiting species
Producing flowers and fruit requires a great deal of energy, and any interruption to growth will sap the tree's strength and reduce its ability to perform for you. For this reason it is best to include extra organic matter or clay, to increase the reservoir for nutrients, and to use a fairly deep pot.

Pots

A bonsai pot is more than just a container for the plant to grow in. It as an integral part of the composition and must complement the tree to form a harmonious unit. Here we show you a selection of different types of pot and indicate what styles or species they best suit.

As well as the aesthetic considerations the pot also has to satisfy some practical requirements, so the following points should be remembered when buying pots:

- Ensure the pot is stoneware, which is frost-proof, as opposed to earthenware, which is not. Earthenware pots will rapidly disintegrate with the first hard frost. A simple test is to wet the unglazed surface of the pot to see if it absorbs the water. If it does it is earthenware, if the water wipes off cleanly the pot is stoneware.

- There must be excellent drainage. The holes should be at least three times greater in number and size than in a conventional flower pot.

- The floor of the pot must be level, so that no pockets of water can accumulate in the base. Check that there are no indentations in the corners where the feet are fixed.

- All pots must have feet in order to leave space for the drained water to flow away.

- Avoid pots which are glazed on the inside. This provides an inhospitable surface for the roots and will cause the soil to dry out too quickly around the perimeter of the pot.

A number of nurseries now sell pots made of mica, which retail at less than half the price of stoneware pots. These look authentic, and are ideal for temporary or training pots, but the surface scratches easily, so they are unsuitable for exhibiting.

Above: *Japanese beech, fagus crenata, are grown for their startling white bark, and are a favourite subject for group plantings.*

Below: *Mame pots, although only tiny, are similar in shape and quality to the full sized ones, although they tend to be more colourful. The art of the mame potter is so appreciated by some enthusiasts that they become collectors' items in their own right, even though they may never be used.*

Right: *The subtle blue glaze on this rectangular pot would especially suit heavy-trunked flowering species such as azalea or quince.*

Above: *Sturdy, cream-glazed ovals like this look good with maples and elms. They are too delicate for strong conifer images.*

Right: *The subtle grey-green glaze on this elegant rectangle would suit most broadleaved species and styles, and could look good with informal, upright larches too.*

Above: *Strong, flared, unglazed rectangle, suitable for heavy-trunked conifers, especially driftwood styes.*

Below: *Very shallow oval glazed pot, designed specifically with group plantings in mind.*

Below: *This superb cascade pot was made in the UK by Derek Aspinall, one of the increasing number of fine western ceramic artists turning their attentions to bonsai pots.*

Above: *Standard brown, unglazed Kobi-ware rectangle. If in doubt, this type of pot will do for almost anything.*

Below: *This shallow, elegant, round pot in a gentle unglased grey, would suit 'feminine' styles such as literati, or thin-trunked deciduous clumps.*

Above: *This 'drum' style pot is made in a variety of sizes and is best used for strong-trunked literati or formal upright styles. It could also be successfully used for heavy clumps.*

5 THE CLASSIC BONSAI STYLES

The main aim of bonsai is to create a tree-like form in miniature. This can be anything from a precise replica of a classic parkland beech to the image of a gnarled and weather-beaten mountain-top juniper, which can be almost abstract in its design.

There is an infinite variety of tree shapes in nature which are imitated in bonsai. It would be impractical, even impossible, to name all of these styles individually, so over the centuries the Japanese devised a number of general classifications. They formalised these and defined a number of classic styles, each having its own distinct aesthetic rules. These govern the shape, angle and proportion of the trunk, number of trunks and location of branches etc.

Although it is only very rarely possible to follow these rules to the letter, tradition states that they should be aspired to at all times. Having said this, it is also true that many of the most admired bonsai in the world break the rules in some way.

I personally prefer a more relaxed and inspirational approach to bonsai, reflecting the more liberal western approach to life in general. However, the rules governing the classic styles are extremely useful to know since they enable bonsai enthusiasts to describe their trees to one another, and they help the beginner to create an aesthetically pleasing design without unnecessary frustration.

Once you have gained a little experience you can break the rules at will and let your own creativity run free.

Right: This stunning informal upright Black pine (Pinus thunbergii), owned by Peter Chan, is a classic example of the style. Note the off-centre placement in the pot.

直幹

FORMAL UPRIGHT STYLE – *CHOKKAN*
As the name implies, this is the most formalised of all styles. The trunk must be ramrod straight and bolt upright, tapering uniformly from base to tip. The branches should be arranged alternately either side of the trunk with every third branch to the rear. The branches should diminish in thickness and in length from the lowest one upwards, and should be either horizontal or sloping downwards.

模様木

INFORMAL UPRIGHT – *MOYOGI*
This is a variation on the formal upright style but is much easier to create. The rules for the branch structure are the same but the trunk may have any number of curves, both from left to right and from front to back. The branches should ideally grow from the outside of the curves and never on the inside as this creates a shock to the eye. The apex should lean towards the front. The illustration shows the ideal form, but any number of variations are perfectly acceptable.

斜幹

SLANTING – *SHAKAN*
Another variation on the formal upright style, except that it is not upright. The trunk is usually straight-ish, although it may have a gentle curve or two. The placement of the branches needs to be carefully thought out in order to stabilise the design and to prevent the tree looking as if it is about to fall over.

WINDSWEPT – *FUKINAGASHI*
Although this is one of the more naturalistic styles, it is also one of the most dramatic. The aim is to capture the dynamic shape and movement of a tree living high in the mountains or on a clifftop, where it is constantly exposed to high prevailing winds. There are no rules governing the trunk shape or location of branches, but in spite of this freedom this is one of the most difficult styles to create successfully.

吹流

One of the outstanding features of this tree is the strong surface root formation.

半懸崖

SEMI-CASCADE – *HAN-KENGAI*
Both this style and the cascade style (overleaf) depict trees clinging to a cliff face, where they are beaten by snow, wind and rockfalls. The trunk should have dramatic curves and taper, and the branches should ideally also cascade from the trunk.
Tradition states that the inverted 'apex' should be directly below the centre of the trunk. The one unbreakable rule is that the lowest point must be below the rim of the pot, but not its base.

41

CASCADE – *KENGAI*
懸崖
The difference between this style and the semi-cascade is that here the trunk must fall below the base of the pot. All other criteria are the same. Good cascades are rare because of the difficulty in maintaining vigour in the lower parts of the tree, opposing its natural urge to grow upwards.

BROOM – *HÔKIDACHI*
箒立
This style was modelled on the natural habit of the zelkova and is seldom successfully used for other than related species, since it works best with trees bearing alternate foliage. All branches should emerge from the top of a straight trunk and fork at regularly diminishing intervals until a network of fine shoots at the tips forms an even-domed crown.

姿婆幹
DRIFTWOOD – *SHARIMIKI*
Echoing the natural appearance of mountain junipers, which produce areas of bare, sun-bleached wood as they age, this style is seldom successfully created from other species. The focal point is the beautiful and dramatic shapes of the grain in the exposed wood. These shapes may be natural but are more often elaborately carved and then bleached and preserved with lime-sulphur. The foliage masses, although acknowledging some of the rules of other styles, serve more as a foil or frame to the driftwood.

文 人 木
LITERATI – *BUNJINGI*
This style is reminiscent of ancient pines, which tend to shed their lower branches as they get old. It gets its name from the calligraphic style of ancient Chinese artists. The focal point of the design is the trunk, so it should be full of character. The branches are limited to the uppermost part of the trunk and should bear just enough foliage to keep the tree healthy and vigorous.

Right: *Pyracantha make very attractive bonsai, especially when the rather feminine beauty of the flowers and fruit are contrasted with the more masculine styles like cascade or this root-over-rock.*

A high potash fertiliser encourages flowers and fruit.

石上樹

ROOT-OVER-ROCK – *SEKIJÔJU*
In rocky terrain the scarce soil is constantly being eroded, exposing the rocks and the roots of the trees growing amongst them. This style depicts such a tree whose roots, as they thicken, cling to any rocks beneath them. The tree itself can be of any style, although broom and formal upright styles look out of place. The most important factor is that the roots should cling tightly to the rock and should have a mature texture.

石付

ROOT-ON-ROCK – *ISHITSUKI*
The tree itself may follow any style, the significance is that a rock is used instead of a pot, with the roots growing in a crevice or hollow. The rock may stand in a shallow dish of soil or, better still, in a water tray. Mixed plantings of pines with red maples or dwarf quince and azalea are particularly successful.

Roots need to be buried for many years to become as thick as these.

43

根連

Right: *This clump-style Japanese red maple breaks one rule by having an even number of trunks. Nevertheless it is a fine example which looks as good in winter as it does in full leaf.*

SINUOUS RAFT – NETSUNANARI

As the name suggests, this is a raft planting where the original horizontal trunk has attractive, snake-like curves and is exposed to show this feature to its best advantage. It is even acceptable for the old trunk to be above the ground in places. The individual trees may follow any style.

筏吹

STRAIGHT RAFT – IKADABUKI

Another obvious one: a raft planting where the original trunk lies in a straight line. Most rafts created from nursery stock follow this style because of the difficulty of bending a fairly thick trunk into sinuous curves. In such cases the trunk is usually buried in the soil or covered with moss to disguise its unnatural appearance.

根上

EXPOSED ROOT – *NEAGARI*
Most of us have driven down country lanes where the steep banks either side have been washed away to expose the roots of ancient beech or pine, and this style is based on such cases. The roots, which must have mature bark and interesting shapes, add a dramatic, rugged appearance, so the design of the tree itself should echo this.

蟠幹

雙樹

TWIN TRUNK – *SÔJU*
Two trunks, one smaller than the other, joined together at the base. Trunks which divide significantly above the base are unacceptable. The smaller or secondary trunk should be slightly to the rear of the dominant one to enhance the perspective. The trees themselves may follow any appropriate style.

TWISTED TRUNK – *BANKAN*
This most unnatural of all bonsai styles has heavy Chinese influence. It became popular for a time earlier this century and was grown in large numbers. Although still popular among some hobbyists, it is seldom accepted in classic circles. The trunk spirals from base to apex while the branch structure follows that of the informal upright.

CLUMP – *KABUDACHI*
株立
Any (odd) number of trunks, which must be in a variety of sizes, all growing on the same roots. This may either be created from suckers (shoots arising naturally from the roots) or by cutting off a thick trunk at the base and using the new shoots which spring up from the stump. The trees can be any style. The horticultural advantage of using a clump rather than separate plants is that the 'trees' do not compete for water and nutrients.

寄植

GROUP – *YOSE-UE*
This style may incorporate any number of trunks from seven up to as many as you like. The main interest is in the interplay between the trunks, which should be of different sizes and should be arranged to give the impression of depth and perspective. No three trunks should form a straight line and no trunk should be obscured by another when viewed from the front.

OTHERS
Other bonsai classes relate to size: Shohin are up to ten inches or so tall, and Mame, or miniature bonsai, are defined as 'being able to sit comfortably in the palm of the hand'.

45

BASIC TECHNIQUES

Repotting and root pruning

The thought of root pruning fills most bonsai novices with horror, but it is essential in order to maintain the tree's health and vigour. If the process is ignored your bonsai will become pot bound. It will weaken, shed shoots and branches and eventually die.

Why prune the roots?
In the wild a tree will extend its roots each growing season in much the same way as it produces new shoots. These new roots do most of the work, absorbing water and nutrients. As the tree matures some older roots will die back, only to be replaced by strong, new ones.

However, things are different in a pot. You have to reproduce this cycle artificially in order to keep your bonsai healthy. Health means vigour, and a vigorous tree is more able to resist disease and can outgrow attacks by pests. It will also respond better to training techniques.

A healthy young bonsai – say up to ten years old – in a small pot will pack its container with roots within one season, so it will need to be root pruned each year. Older trees, especially conifers, tend to grow more slowly, taking perhaps up to five years to fill the pot. However, before you start to panic, remember that it takes time for problems associated with root confinement to take effect, and you can miss a year every so often without putting your tree at risk.

When to root prune
Just as the roots begin to grow in spring is the ideal time for root pruning. Although it is possible to repot at any time during the dormant season, the longer the wounds wait before they can regenerate,

1 After two years, the roots of this medium-size trident maple are filling the pot, and need to be pruned. They are all healthy, and as you can see, they have already started to grow. The fine, white vertical roots are from weed seeds which germinated over the winter.

2 Lift the tree from its pot and carefully comb out the roots. Work from the centre outwards. Use a chopstick, knitting needle, or whatever else comes to hand.

3 Comb out the underneath of the root mass as well, without tearing them. When you have finished you should have removed about a third of the total volume of soil.

4 Trim the roots back so that the remaining root mass doesn't quite fill the pot. Use a sharp pair of scissors, but not your best ones, because of the grit in the soil!

2 Push the wire through the mesh and drainage holes and bend the 'legs' up tight against the underneath of the pot.

5 Cover the grit with a layer of fresh soil. This must be well sifted to remove all the fine particles. Make a small mound of soil where the trunk will sit.

1 You can repot the tree in the same container, or in a more suitable one as we are doing. First, cover the drainage holes with mesh, held in place with wire loops like these.

5 It is important to trim the roots underneath as well, otherwise the tree will rise in its pot as it grows. Thick roots should be pruned hard back to encourage compact growth.

3 Some pots have additional small holes for tie wires. If not, you can use the drainage holes. You need at least two pieces of wire to make the tree secure until the roots have re-established.

4 Cover the floor of the pot with coarse grit to aid drainage. If the pot is less than an inch deep you do not need a drainage course, provided the soil is sufficiently free-draining.

the more they are at risk of further damage from frost and fungal attack.

The exact timing depends on the advancement of the season, geographical location and the species. Deciduous trees, particularly trident maples and elms, start producing new roots as early as mid-February in the south of England but not until a month later in the north. Pines may not start new root growth in earnest until April in the south and as late as May further north.

The first sign of root activity is a slight swelling of the buds on last year's shoots. You can check further by gently lifting the tree from its pot and taking a close look at the roots. If the tips appear to be swelling the time is right. If the tips are white they have already started to grow, but pruning will do them no harm so long as the new buds have not opened yet.

If, on the other hand, your tree is due for repotting in theory and the buds have begun to swell but the visible roots appear brown and dead, this may be an indication of decay. You should therefore repot immediately, following the steps outlined in *Emergency repotting*, below.

It is a good idea to inspect the roots of all your bonsai periodically, whether they are due for root pruning or not. This is particularly important if the tree is looking a bit off colour. As often as not, lack of vigour, wilting or premature leaf-fall is a symptom of a root-related problem such as decay or attack by the voracious vine weevil larva (*see page 110*).

After repotting wait two weeks before heavy pruning, and delay feeding for four to six weeks, or until new growth has been established.

Emergency repotting
Sometimes it is necessary to repot a tree 'out of season'. An emergency is likely when you inspect the roots of an ailing tree and notice they are decaying, or worse still, missing! This may be due to fungal attack, most likely resulting from poor drainage or over feeding. or to the appetite of a subterranean pest. In either instance the following action should be taken:

• Defoliate all deciduous trees to reduce water loss. Do not defoliate evergreens.

• *Very gently* comb away all the dead roots and soil. Then, equally gently, hose away all the remaining soil. Inspect what is left thoroughly, remove any larvae and remaining dead roots. Don't cut any living roots if you can help it.

• Plant the tree straight away in an oversized container, using a soil mix of at least eighty percent grit *and no loam*. Bury the roots deeper than before and water, using a solution of systemic fungicide.

• Place the tree in an 'intensive care unit' – either a humid, but ventilated poly-tunnel, or home-made polythene tent, and spray at least once a day.

• Maintain an evenly damp soil. There should be just enough moisture to satisfy the tree's reduced needs but little enough to encourage the roots to grow in search of more. Using the extra gritty soil helps achieve this balance. Do not feed until the tree has fully recovered.

1 Nestle the tree into the mound of soil, placing it just off-centre, for best aesthetic effect, with the surface of the root mass just below the pot's rim.

2 Next pull the wire ties down over the root mass and twist them together until the tree does not rock. Cushion the bark with squares of rubber or foam.

Right: Our newly-repotted tree now needs to be placed in a sheltered position until new growth starts. It should not be watered again until really necessary, and not fed for four weeks, to avoid burning the tender new roots.

This is an ideal time to do the odd bit of wiring.

Note how last year's shoots have been pruned to an outward-facing bud.

3 Fill the remaining spaces with fresh soil. If the soil is virtually dry it is a lot easier to apply, because it runs freely and does not compact as you work it into the empty spaces.

4 Work the soil in between the roots, ensuring that there are no air pockets. Traditionalists recommend using a chopstick, but fingers are more sensitive, and nearer to hand.

5 Water the newly potted tree well, but use a fine rose or spray, so you don't wash away the new soil. Repeat the operation a few minutes later to ensure a thorough soaking.

Shaping with wire

Wiring is the most fundamental process in bonsai training, allowing the accurate positioning of branches and shoots. The principle is simple but the skill does take a little time to acquire.

Wire of a suitable gauge is coiled around a branch or shoot. The two can then be bent and manoeuvred into the desired position, and the wire will hold the branch in place. After a period of growth has taken place, the branch will set in that position and the wire can be removed (see page 52).

The time taken for this to happen varies from one species to another. Conifers, especially junipers, may take several years to set, during which time the wire may need to be removed and reapplied several times to avoid damaging the bark. Some deciduous species may set in a matter of a few weeks.

Older, stiffer branches will also take longer, and you may have to bend them little by little every few weeks until the desired position is achieved. Every plant is an individual, and it is only with experience that you will learn just how far you can go before snapping the branch, so take it easy at first.

Before you embark on your first wiring exercise you should practise the technique on a twig or branch from a garden shrub, preferably a species similar to the one you have chosen for your bonsai. See how thick the wire needs to be, and how far the branch will bend without breaking.

The branches on this old 'shimpaku' juniper from Japan would have been wired into position many years ago, while they were young and flexible.

2 *When you bend the branch, do it gradually. Spread your hands so you hold as much of the branch as possible and use both thumbs as leverage points.*

3 *Once bent, the wire should hold the branch in position. If the branch springs back, the wire is too thin, if it cuts the bark, it is too tight.*

1 *For your first try, use fairly thick wire which is easier to handle. Always hold the wired part of the branch firmly with one hand and coil the wire with the other.*

What wire?

Custom made aluminium wire is readily available from all bonsai outlets and by mail order. This is anodised to give it an unobtrusive brown finish, and although it is suitable for most purposes it can be expensive. (For this book we decided to use silver aluminium wire, which is also available from most bonsai retailers, because it shows up better in the photographs.)

The Japanese traditionally use copper wire for conifers because its superior holding power is more effective on their springier branches. If aluminium wire is used it needs to be much thicker and is therefore more unsightly.

Plastic-coated iron wire is sold in two thicknesses in garden centres and can be used as a last resort, but is too stiff and consequently more difficult to apply safely. What's more, if this wire is used on junipers and the plastic coating splits, allowing the metal contact with broken bark, it can react with the cambium, turning it into

4 When wiring long branches, reduce the thickness of the wire as the branch diameter decreases. Overlap the different thicknesses by two or three turns.

CORRECT WIRING

The example on the left shows the coils too close together. This reduces the holding power and restricts the sap flow.

On the right, the coils are too far apart and would have very little holding power.

The example in the centre shows ideal wiring. The coils are at approximately 45 degrees.

6 The best plan is to use one piece of wire for two branches, which provides perfect anchorage. Coil the wire in the directions shown here.

5 When wiring a side branch, anchor the wire by coiling it around the trunk. Always take it through the fork of the branch as shown.

7 It is also best to use one piece of wire for forked branches. Make sure you coil it in opposite directions on each branch, otherwise the wire on the first branch will uncoil as you work on the second one.

51

a black, decaying mess, and causing the branch to die back. If allowed to remain on the branch for more than a week or two, the effect may even prove fatal to the tree.

How thick?

With a little experience you will soon be able to assess what gauge of wire will be needed for any given branch. You may need to use two pieces of wire for heavy branches, but remember that this will only increase the holding power by about fifty percent. On the other hand, doubling the thickness will increase the holding power by a factor of three.

How much?

Plan your wiring 'strategy' in advance. Decide where you want the wiring to begin and end, and cut a piece at least a third longer than the length of the branch. If you are going to use twin wires use one piece doubled up. Start by anchoring the end where the pieces are joined and work them both together along the branch.

Finally, if you are unhappy with your first live attempt, carefully remove the wire by cutting it off and have another go.

CLAMPS

Sometimes you may want to create a sharp bend, or alter the direction of a really thick branch or trunk, where no amount of wire would have any effect.

In such cases special clamps like this can be employed. They are available in a variety of sizes, the largest one being capable of bending a conifer branch over one inch thick.

Care must be taken to cushion the bark against the considerable pressure applied by the clamp. Avoid trying to create too severe a bend in one go – it is much better to give the clamp an extra turn every week or so until the desired position is reached.

1 A plan view of a fully wired deciduous branch. Note how the side branches are fanned out like spread fingers, and how straight lines are avoided.

2 Side view of the same branch. It is important to build height on the branches of deciduous trees, as well as width. There is plenty of space between each shoot for future growth.

3 Pine branches are wired to a different shape. The side branches should cascade slightly from the main limb, forming a low dome. The tip of each shoot is wired to point upwards.

4 *A plan view of a juniper branch, shaped in the traditional way for the formal upright style. Note the triangular shape and how the side branches are positioned alternately.*

On junipers and pines, stripping old foliage like this allows light to stimulate back budding. For some curious reason, the wire itself also seems to have a similar affect.

REMOVING WIRE

Wire can be expensive, so it is tempting to unwind it once it has served its purpose, in order to use it another time. However, this is a risky business since it is much easier to damage the bark, or even snap the branch, when working in reverse. The branch will have swollen so the wire will be tighter than when you first applied it, and will naturally be full of kinks, making it difficult to manipulate.

It is much safer to snip the wire away using wire cutters which cut right up to the tip of the jaws. Custom-made Japanese bonsai wire cutters are designed for this purpose, but can be quite expensive. To start with, good quality electrical wire cutters will do the job just as well if you choose the tool carefully. You will need the long-handled type to enable you to reach awkward places. Any damage to the bark caused by the cutters will be superficial and will heal much quicker than damage caused through careless uncoiling.

If you are worried about the unnecessary expense of 'wasting' wire in this way, ask yourself this question: what is the most valuable to you, a few inches of wire or a developing bonsai which you have laboured over for hours and nurtured for years?

5 *If the wire stays on too long it will cut right into the bark like this. Remove it in good time and, if the branch hasn't set, rewire it, coiling in the opposite direction.*

Branch pruning

When a branch is pruned it will inevitably leave a scar. With full-sized trees the wound will normally heal rapidly and any resulting disfiguration will be of little or no consequence.

However, since bonsai grow more slowly the healing process is slower as well, so it needs all the help it can get. Also great care must be taken to minimise the possibility of unsightly swellings around the wound, and to encourage the scar to blend in with the character of the trunk.

The first technique shows you how to execute simple pruning, where a small to medium sized branch is removed. The second shows how to use a larger wound to your advantage, by hollowing it out and turning it into an interesting feature.

Here are a few general points to bear in mind:

• Always use very sharp tools, which should ideally be sterilised by immersing them in methylated spirit for a few minutes. This is especially important when pruning away diseased wood.

• The cambium layer (between the bark and the heartwood) must be sealed against frost, water and drying wind. If left exposed it may die back, increasing the size of the wound and delaying the healing process.

• Never use horticultural bitumen-based sealants. These will dry hard and will be impossible to remove from the surrounding bark without causing disfiguration.

• Feed the tree well after drastic pruning to speed up the healing process. The more vigorous the tree, the quicker it will heal.

• Any unwanted shoots which arise from around the wound must be rubbed off as soon as they appear. Failure to do this will result in swellings around the scar, causing even more disfiguration.

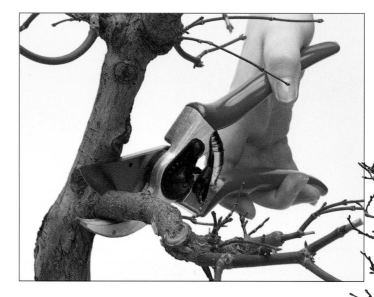

1 If you don't have any bonsai tools some sharp secateurs will do. Use the 'bypass' type rather than the 'anvil' type, and make sure the non-cutting blade is furthest from the trunk.

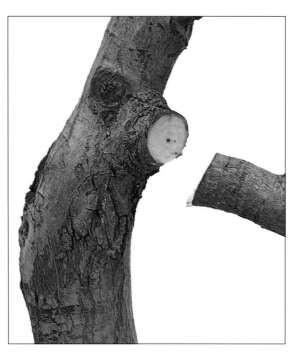

2 Leave a small stub at first, rather than attempting to cut right up to the trunk. It is so easy to damage the bark on the trunk if you are too impatient.

3 If you do have special branch pruners, use them to finish off the cut as close to the trunk as possible. It will heal more neatly if you create a slight hollow in the exposed wood.

DISGUISING LARGE WOUNDS

Sometimes it is necessary to prune away really heavy branches, causing scars which would normally take many years to heal. Even then, they might be too large to be in proportion with the rest of the bonsai.

You can turn these large scars to your advantage by hollowing out the wound, right through to the heartwood. If carried out with care this can result in a natural looking feature which will add age and character to the trunk.

You can make the hollow as deep as you like, since the heartwood is essentially dead, so long as the sapwood and cambium are intact.

Above: You need to use very sharp gouges or routers when carving.
Right: This hollow trunk has acquired all the character of an ancient tree.

While developing this English elm bonsai it was necessary to prune a branch in the front of the trunk. This practice should be avoided if at all possible as the scar will be in the most noticable place of all. However, after six or seven years the wound has now healed over nicely and is beginning to blend with the surronding bark.

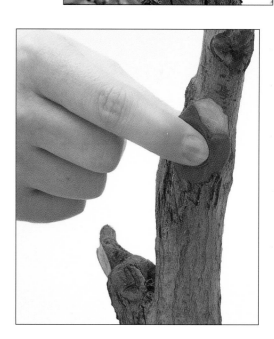

4 Clean up the edges of the wound with a very sharp knife. Ragged edges heal unevenly and are likely to harbour fungal spores which may later infect the whole tree.

5 Seal the wound thoroughly, especially around the edges. If you don't have any special bonsai sealant, try mixing a little olive oil with grafting wax or children's modelling clay.

Maintenance pruning

It takes many hours each winter to carry out maintenance pruning on this trident maple in order to keep the fine twig structure.

Each year your bonsai will throw out new shoots from the buds created in the leaf axils during the previous growing season. It will only take a few weeks for these shoots to outgrow the design of the tree and make it look very scruffy.

In a developing or semi-mature bonsai these shoots can be allowed to grow to six or seven leaves before they are cut back. Allowing them this period of free growth thickens the parent branches and trunk and builds up a general vigour in the tree. If allowed to grow too long they will sap the strength from the finer growth and will quickly kill it off. New shoots will emerge from the buds in the remaining leaf axils. Any wayward shoots, or those which are destined to become new branches, should be wired at this stage.

However, in established bonsai this annual growth will need to be cut back during the dormant season to allow the next season's growth room to extend before outgrowing the design. Over the seasons this constant 'clip-and-grow' technique will reward you with a much-forked branch structure, with all the characteristics of an ancient tree.

Here we show how to approach the winter pruning of trees with alternate and opposite leaves – in this case English elm and Japanese maple. Always remember to prune to a bud which points in the direction you want the new growth to take. It is possible to style a bonsai entirely by pruning if you have the patience.

The best time to do your winter pruning is late in the season, before the buds swell but after the worst of the weather is over. The setback to the tree caused by pruning off fattening buds is slight. But prolonged periods of frost could do severe damage to a newly-pruned bonsai.

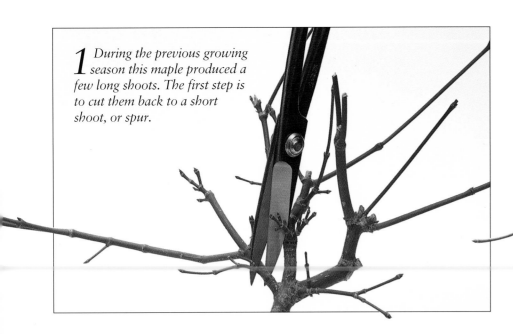

1 During the previous growing season this maple produced a few long shoots. The first step is to cut them back to a short shoot, or spur.

2 Every few years it is necessary to prune away older growth to prevent overcrowding and to maintain neat foliage pads.

5 *Like the maple, this elm has grown some long shoots which need to be pruned first.*

6 *Unwanted shoots arising from older wood should also be cut off. Notice the stage of bud development. This is an ideal time for maintenance pruning, since you can easily see where all the minute buds are located.*

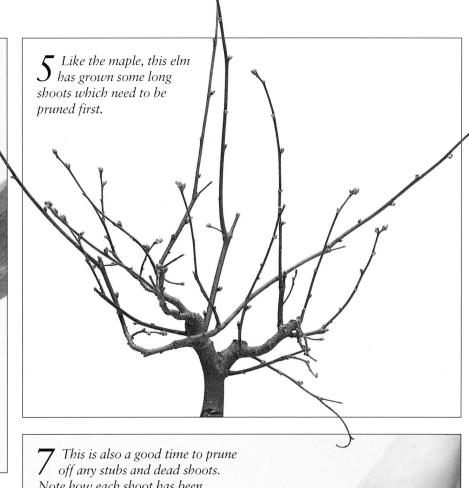

3 *Finally, cut back all spurs to one or two buds. You may have to look quite closely to see the buds because they can be minute. Look carefully at the base of each spur.*

7 *This is also a good time to prune off any stubs and dead shoots. Note how each shoot has been pruned to a bud facing in the direction the new growth is required.*

8 *Each of the remaining shortened shoots bears dormant buds around its base, which will sprout in the future, thus ensuring a never ending supply of new shoots. These will eventually grow and replace the shoots you see here, which will then be pruned away. And so the cycle continues ....*

4 *After a good prune the branch looks rather naked, but remember that every remaining bud will generate a new shoot next season, producing an ever-more-compact twig structure.*

Summer pinching

Once the branch structure has become established there should be enough new shoots appearing each spring, bearing sufficient foliage to sustain the tree without necessarily allowing any extension growth. Extension growth draws the energy from the rest of the tree, concentrating it in the growing tips. This starves the fine inner twigs of nutrients and the additional foliage prevents them gaining adequate light. The result is that the fine twigs die and the whole twig development process will need to be started all over again.

First we have to build and refine this tracery of fine twigs. Once this has been done the resulting foliage pads must be kept trimmed and in balance with the design. Both these ends are achieved by pinching out the tips of all new growth as it appears.

Different species grow in different ways, and the following techniques have been developed to accommodate the five most common growth patterns.

• With broadleaved trees new shoots will emerge from the buds in the remaining leaf axils.

• In pines new buds will form at the point at which the shoot is pinched, as well as further back on older growth.

• Larch and spruce will only produce new shoots from buds which are already visible on the remaining shoot or from around the base of the shoot and on older growth.

• Junipers will throw out new growth from any branch or shoot which bears foliage, and need constant pinching throughout the growing season.

This magnificent Japanese maple is grown in the unusual split-trunk style. The delicately-coloured spring foliage adopts a pose reminiscent of trees seen in Japanese prints.

1 *Spruce buds open to form tiny, bright green tufts which should be plucked before they have fully elongated. Don't do the whole tree at one go, spread the job over two weeks.*

2 *As pine buds begin to grow they elongate, forming 'candles' which should have up to two thirds snapped off before the needles develop. Twist and bend at the same time.*

3 *Junipers produce prolific new growth, forming tightly-packed foliage. This extension growth is distinguished by its lighter colour. Hold the fan of foliage in one hand and pull out all extending growth with the finger and thumb of the other. With practise, you will be able to pinch quite large bunches of foliage in one go.*

4 *Zelkovas and other alternate-leaved species produce new leaves one at a time at the shoot tips. This leaf, and the minute bud at its base, should be pinched out, using tweezers if necessary.*

5 *Maples produce new leaves in pairs borne on a short extending shoot. Both leaves should be pinched out, together with the tiny developing bud nestled between them.*

Leaf pruning

This is the ultimate refinement technique which is only suitable for broadleaved deciduous species. It results in a very fine, compact twig formation, tiny leaves and enhanced autumn colour in the year it is applied. Leaf pruning can also be employed as a device for reducing transpiration after emergency out-of-season repotting *(see page 48)*.

Since this technique causes a certain amount of stress to the tree it should only be carried out every three years or so, and only on trees which are in good health and vigour. For this reason its use is normally restricted to bonsai which are in preparation for exhibition. The ideal time for leaf pruning is early summer, as soon as the spring growth has hardened.

The principle is similar to shoot pruning and pinching, in that the reduction of foliage encourages new side growth to take place. But because the foliage is totally removed the tree undergoes a 'false autumn' and next year's growth develops this year. This means that there will be a much greater number of new shoots than existed before, bearing correspondingly more leaves.

Since the tree can only support – and only requires – a fixed volume of foliage, these leaves will be greatly reduced in size. Also, since these leaves only have half a season to live they will be in better condition come autumn, resulting in brighter colour over a longer period.

1 This shohin field maple received a merit award from Saburo Kato, president of the World Bonsai Federation. Being small, it needs regular leaf pruning to reduce the scale of the leaves.

2 Even though it may seem a little unnerving at first, take the plunge and start snipping off all the leaves, one by one.

3 Cut just below the leaf, leaving the petiole, or leaf stalk, intact. This prevents excessive 'bleeding'.

4 Leaf pruning also presents an ideal opportunity to check the progress of the branch structure. The petioles which remain on the tree will fall as soon as the new leaves start to emerge

5 After a week or two the new crop of leaves emerges, brighter and even more colourful than in the first flush of spring.

6 Less than a month later the tree has grown a full crop of small, brightly-coloured leaves, borne on short shoots.

61

First steps: cuttings

Seedlings and cuttings are free and easy to come by, so they are ideal material for your first attempts at creating bonsai. If the result is not too good it doesn't really matter, you will probably have other plants ready to replace the initial failure. If, on the other hand, the result is satisfactory you will have a bonsai that will improve as time goes by with the right care and attention.

We have repotted this cutting to complete the demonstration. You should ideally wait until the following spring, to allow the plant time to regain strength.

Whatever species you choose, seedling or cutting, the plant should be growing vigorously before you attempt any pruning or wiring.

For this sequence we selected a two-year-old cutting of a juniper, *Juniperus squamata meyerii*, because its compact foliage enables us to create an almost instant bonsai. With deciduous species you will have to build up the shape over two or three years.

Here are a few points to remember:

• Don't let the plant dictate the eventual size of the bonsai. Lok for the 'tree within'.

• Where a trunk forks use the thinnest one as the leader to enhance trunk taper.

• Leave as many branches as possible to keep the tree vigorous, you can always prune them again in years to come.

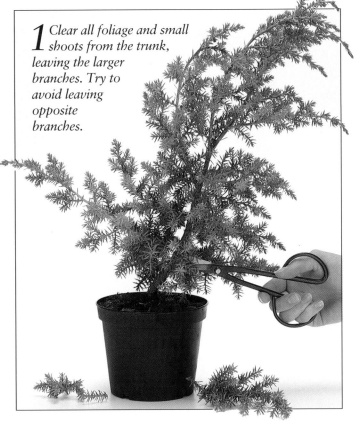

1 Clear all foliage and small shoots from the trunk, leaving the larger branches. Try to avoid leaving opposite branches.

2 Don't let the size of the original plant dictate the eventual size of the bonsai. Here we are cutting off one of the twin leaders, leaving a side shoot to form a branch.

3 The other leader is now shortened. This time a side shoot is left to become the new leader. Working this way, we are increasing trunk taper, making the tree appear older.

4 To start wiring the trunk, take a sturdy piece of wire and anchor it by pushing it into the soil close to the trunk. Find a spot where you will not damage any roots.

7 Grasp as much of the trunk as possible to spread the pressure and bend it into the desired shape. Introduce some curves from front to back as well as from side to side.

5 Hold the trunk and wire together firmly and begin to coil. Hold close to the point where you are coiling and move your hand along the trunk as you progress.

8 Bend the branches down, making sure there are a few at the back. Bend close to the trunk. Clear any growth facing downwards.

6 Next wire the branches, using one piece of wire for two branches, as described on page 50. Wire right to the tip of each branch.

After a couple of hours our juniper already looks like a little tree. As time passes the trunk will thicken and the foliage pads will fill out. Low branches will be pruned and others allowed to extend as the shape is gradually developed and refined.

First steps: seedlings

Nowadays most bonsai are created by reducing larger plants or by growing branches onto pre-formed trunks. However, there is still a very important place for growing bonsai straight from seed. It helps you to learn about the growth patterns of each species and makes you more aware of the structure of trees. But most importantly, by growing bonsai from seed you can create an almost perfect little tree on a very small scale, without the need for heavy pruning scars, jins, and so on. Being able to display a tiny, unblemished and well-formed bonsai that you grew from seed is a most satisfying and rewarding achievement.

Having pricked out your seedling as described on page 25, let it grow on unchecked for the rest of the season, since it is important to have an established root system before you begin training. The following year, during late spring/early summer, or as soon as the new growth has hardened off, you can make the first pruning cut. The purpose of this cut is to force the seedling to produce side branches, and it is the most drastic pruning you will ever need to do. Once the new branches have grown a little you can carry out the initial wiring as shown here.

You can plant your fledgeling bonsai in a shallow but oversized container at the beginning of its third growing season. From now on, year after year, the continuing process of painstakingly wiring new shoots into position and regularly pinching out growing tips will gradually produce an incredibly realistic branch structure bearing a crop of tiny leaves.

• It is essential not to hurry the process. Remember that you are 'building' the final shape of the tree in much the same way as nature does. The longer you take to achieve the final shape the better the result will be.

• Try to plan the final size and shape of the bonsai in advance and pinch back to buds which will send the new growth in the desired direction.

• Never let run-away shoots grow out of control. They will thicken the parent branch out of proportion with the others and ruin the design. They will then have to be pruned and re-grown.

• Let new shoots put on three or four leaf nodes and then pinch back hard. If you try to grow each branch to its final intended length too soon it will not produce any forks.

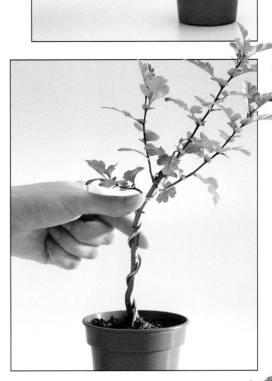

1 This typical hawthorn seedling is just beginning its third summer. It is pruned back to just three tiny spurs. Note the position and angle of the cut.

2 After three months the spurs have become strong shoots. Two will become branches, and the third the new leader. Anchor the wire in the soil before coiling it around the trunk.

3 Now the trunk can be shaped. Bend from back to front as well as from side to side, avoiding exaggerated curves.

Snipping off the apex encourages more branches to form.

6 Over the years the triangular shape will be allowed to become more rounded, as each bud throws out a new shoot which, in turn, can become another branch.

4 The branches have been wired, spread evenly around the trunk and lowered to a horizontal position, and the trunk has a series of diminishing curves.

This eighteen-year-old hawthorn was grown in exactly the same way as demonstrated here. The bark was encouraged to crack and flake by wrapping it with loose, wet sphagnum moss for a year.

5 Shortening the stronger branches encourages new ones to form, as well as promoting side growth on the remaining ones. The aim is for a triangular outline at this stage.

Garden centre plants: Cotoneatser

One of my favourite species for bonsai is Cotoneaster. The tiny leaves are dark, glossy green, they bear minute pink-white flowers in spring and the bright red berries stay on the plant from late summer right through the winter. Some varieties, like *horizontalis*, which we have chosen here, are deciduous, giving the added bonus of autumn golds and reds. The growth is symmetrical and entirely predictable, producing a herring-bone pattern of branches and twigs – ideal for bonsai training into almost any style.

Garden centre plants tend to be well fed and watered but they live fairly close together. This encourages long, vigorous shoots which we are going to use to our advantage in this exercise by creating a cascade style.

Because it is against the tree's nature to grow downwards it will channel more energy to the crown at the expense of the tip of the cascade. To compensate for this you should select a vigorous branch for the cascade and keep the top well thinned out. Spray foliar feed on the lower parts regularly and only use a soil fertiliser sparingly.

It is quite common for extreme cascades to be laid on their backs for much of the time and only to be stood upright for watering. This can also help counter the tree's compulsion to grow upwards, but it does have disadvantages. The pot may not drain too well in this position and the leaves will turn to face the light, so they look odd when the bonsai is the right way up. It takes a day or two for the leaves to re-adjust to their normal position.

1 This cotoneaster is typical of garden centre stock, with strong branches growing in all directions, but no discernable trunk. By tilting it to one side, its potential for a cascade style becomes apparent.

2 The essence of a good cascade style is to make the trunk begin its cascade as close to the base as possible, so it is cut right back to the lowest pair of heavy branches.

3 One remaining branch becomes the new leader and the other is shortened to form a low, stunted crown.

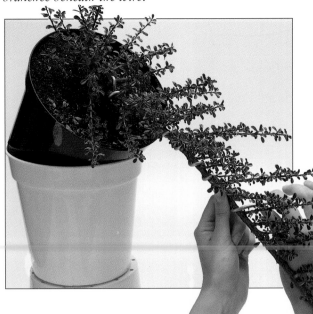

4 Rub off cluttered shoots and wire the new trunk from base to tip, taking care not to crush any small branches beneath the wire.

5 Make the bends in the trunk as sharp as possible, reflecting the tortuous conditions suffered by natural cascading trees in the mountains. The bends should be made from front to back as well as from side to side, and should be tighter towards the tip of the trunk.

The deep pot creates a visual and horticultural balance

8 Leave a few short stubs to serve as anchorage points for the wire when you prune. This is kinder to the plant than anchoring the wire round the trunk.

6 When you are satisfied with the trunk line you can decide which side branches to keep. Try to make these emerge from the outside of a bend in the trunk. The trunk should be cleaned of all other shoots and tufts of foliage.

7 The branches should cascade in the same way as the trunk, with similar curves, but on a smaller scale. Note how the sparse branches in the stunted crown also cascade, giving unity to the design.

Cascade style bonsai need to be displayed on tall stands such as this rosewood one from China.

9 Once the tree is planted in a proper cascade pot the final adjustments can be made to the branches. It will now grow away vigorously, especially at the extreme top and bottom, so regular pruning will be needed to keep the foliage pads neat. In time more branches may be pruned.

Garden centre plants: Cedar

The Literati style, although found frequently in nature, gets its name from the fact that the trunk shapes were originally inspired by the brush strokes of ancient Chinese scribes. This is the oldest style of bonsai and was established long before it became popular in Japan. It is the original link between horticulture and art.

In nature this style is invariably limited to exposed, mountain conifers such as Scots pine, larch or spruce, which naturally shed lower branches as they mature. Very rarely does one find a literati deciduous tree of any beauty.

The essence of the design is the trunk line, which should have taper and should present many changes of direction. The branches are limited to the uppermost portion of the trunk and foliage is kept to a minimum – just sufficient to maintain the tree's health.

In this case we are using a garden centre cedar whose initial attraction was the long lower branch, which eventually becomes the leader. It is amazing how often the removal of most of the trunk, and the selection of a lower branch to take its place, can create ancient-looking and dramatic effects.

Only repot at the same sitting if you're working in spring, otherwise wait until next year.

1 We chose this Atlantic cedar because of the potential offered by the long, low branch.

2 The surface roots of this plant were buried deep in the pot. The tough elastic net, used by the nursery when transplanting, has to be disentangled and cut away.

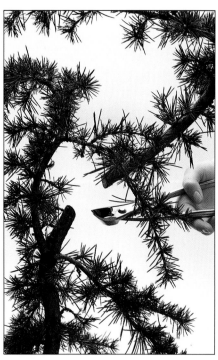

3 The obvious first step is to remove the unwanted upper trunk, leaving a stub to form a jin later. Using a branch as the new leader increases taper and creates a sharp bend.

4 Next the short spurs and tufts of foliage need to be cleaned from the trunk, and the first quarter of each branch. Then you can select which branches to keep and which to prune.

5 The stub of the original trunk is jinned and the trunk and branches are wired. The essence of literati is trunk line and sparse foliage, so only a few branches remain.

6 When shaping the trunk, aim for a combination of sharp bends and gradual curves. Try not to make them predictable, and remember to work in three dimensions, not just two.

8 Fortunately the roots are in excellent condition, as you can see. Because this tree leans considerably, it needs to be wired firmly into the pot.

7 Having established the basic trunk and branch structure, the final tidying up takes place. Any downward-facing buds or shoots must be removed.

The trunk has already swelled, so the wire must soon be replaced.

Final adjustments have been made to the shape of the trunk.

This knot of thick root could become an interesting feature.

Right: Three months later, the tree has put on considerable growth, and has already had its first pinching. As the tree develops, the bottom two (perhaps even four) branches will be removed!

Garden shrub: Juniper

As the name implies, this style is inspired by trees found growing on cliff-tops, where they are shaped by constant exposure to prevailing winds. Although the principles behind the design are simple it can be difficult to arrive at a totally convincing result and much depends on the potential of the raw material.

The most suitable species for this style are conifers, since the foliage pads have cleaner outlines and the growth can be precisely controlled. With deciduous trees the larger leaves face all directions, ruining the effect, particularly on smaller bonsai.

Choose a plant which already has a tendency to grow towards one side, or has one side branch showing potential, which can become the main trunk.

Keep the trunk and the first half to two-thirds of the branch line clear of foliage. In nature winds not only shape the branches, they also strip young shoots and only allow new growth at the tips, where the force of the wind is broken by the rest of the tree.

This process must be imitated by the bonsai artist in the years that follow the initial styling. This will inevitably lead to over-extended growth, so every few years it will be necessary to cut the foliage pads back as far as possible and re-grow them. As a result you will create an ever more angular and battered looking branch structure which will add to the beauty of your bonsai.

Never be afraid to adjust the design as time passes by removing or jinning branches, or creating sharis on the trunk. The more 'damage' you can create on this style of bonsai, the more convincing it will eventually become.

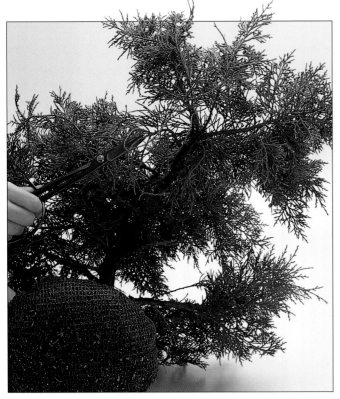

1 This Chinese juniper outgrew its space in a neighbour's rock garden. The root ball is wrapped in netting to keep it intact while we are working out the tree.

2 From underneath the main trunk line is more visible. Start by removing all dead shoots and weak, spindly branches.

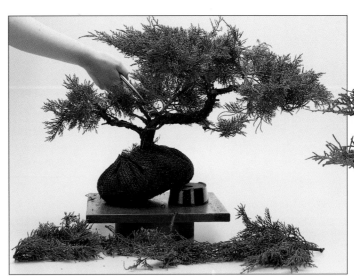

3 The trunkline is now clear, but there's more pruning to do yet. Windswept trees shed branches as they grow, retaining a few on the lee side.

Initial styling is complete. The secondary trunk has gone, as it conflicted with the overall design. Some jins have been shaped with heat (see page 77). From now on the branches will be allowed to extend to the left, without gaining in bulk.

5 *Having wired the remaining branches, they should all be shaped to follow the wind-blown sweep of the trunk, with similar curves, but on a decreasing scale.*

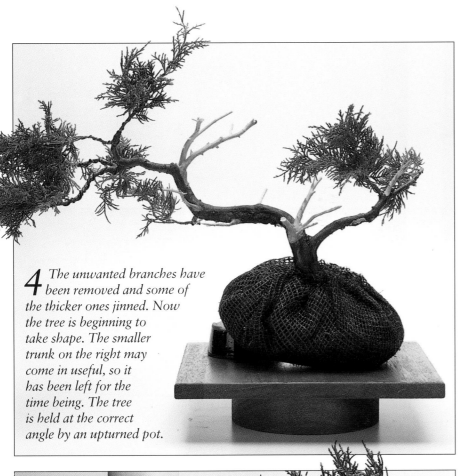

4 *The unwanted branches have been removed and some of the thicker ones jinned. Now the tree is beginning to take shape. The smaller trunk on the right may come in useful, so it has been left for the time being. The tree is held at the correct angle by an upturned pot.*

6 *All downward-facing shoots must now be cut off to emphasise the flowing branch lines, characteristic of the windswept style.*

7 *Note how the foliage pads are being trimmed to a narrow wedge shape – another device to enhance the illusion of a tree which is subjected to strong prevailing winds.*

Home-grown stock: Siberian elm

This is one of the examples on page 30. It is a Siberian elm grown from seed, and had been growing in open ground for six years before being potted up in early spring a year ago. These are vigorous trees and are ideal for this method of styling.

What we are doing here in effect is building a bonsai. We start by developing a good trunk with an interesting line and pronounced taper. The next step is to add the branches. As you can see we have plenty of choice. Many of the older branches are too thick to bend next to the trunk so we will concentrate on the young, thinner ones.

The best time to tackle a project like this is in mid-summer, while the tree still has plenty of time to put on a lot more growth before autumn. If you do it too late in the year the new growth will not be fully hardened before the frosts begin and it will wither. If you try this while the tree is dormant frost may enter the hairline cracks caused when the branches are bent and this may result in die-back of entire branches, which means back to square one!

• When positioning the basic branch structure you should avoid straight lines (unless you are producing a formal upright style) and try to bend the branch at each point where a side shoot emerges. Remember to introduce vertical curves as well as horizontal ones.

• Feed the tree well to encourage new growth but reduce the nitrogen content towards late summer in order to harden off any tender young shoots.

• Allow all the new shoots which emerge from the branches to grow unchecked in order to thicken the host branches.

• Apply the wire fairly loosely because the branches will thicken and set rapidly.

• Check the wiring after three weeks and then every few days after that. As soon as it appears too tight renew it immediately.

• Next spring the long shoots can be pruned back and selected ones wired into position to form the secondary branches. New growth from these should be allowed to extend to six or seven leaf nodes, and then trimmed back to two or three. These, too, can be *loosely* wired into position. Feeding heavily will mean that you will need to repeat this 'grow and clip' cycle several times throughout the season. In a year or two this tree can be planted in a display pot and the refinement stage can begin.

2 After a couple of weeks the remaining shoots have recovered and put on some more growth. Only a few will be trained, the rest will go.

1 Many of these branches are too thick to be of use. They would tend to split away from the trunk when bent. They will be cut off completely; the rest will be shortened.

Below: By the end of the season the foliage pads are developing well. I have changed the 'front', preferring the trunk line from this angle. Next spring I will plant the tree in a proper bonsai pot.

TRAINING GROUND

Finding a concealed corner of the garden for trees in various stages of training is better than cluttering your display area with them. All sorts of temporary containers can be used, from flower pots to my favourite – old washing-up bowls. Drainage holes can be introduced by pushing a red hot pipe through the bottom of the bowl.

Large wounds like this will be hollowed out to add character.

The surface roots are not perfect, but a little carving or thread grafting will soon sort them out.

My automatic leaf pruner. The caterpillar of the comma butterfly does no harm.

3 *Selected shoots are shortened and wired into position. Any over-long side shoots are also shortened to encourage bushy growth. It is a good idea to introduce quite exaggerated curves in the branches at this stage as they will become less pronounced as the branches thicken.*

73

Landscape plant: Scots pine

Most big garden centres, especially those who specialise in landscaping, will stock large container-grown trees and shrubs. These can offer tremendous potential and are, surprisingly, rather easier to work on than you may think at first.

Here we have chosen a variety of Scots pine, *Pinus sylvestris nana*. It has a compact growth pattern, readily throws out buds on old wood and naturally produces very small needles. Other similar varieties are *Beauvronensis* and *Waterii*. Steer clear of varieties which have long needles and coarse growth.

Although Japanese pine bonsai are grown in many styles: literati, cascade, driftwood etc., the vast majority of commercial trees seem to be stocky, thick-trunked informal or formal uprights. These full triangular shapes are more reminiscent of young pine trees in the west. If you look at the pines in your neighbourhood you will discover they have a style all of their own, approaching literati sometimes, but relatively straight-trunked with cascading branches. This is the style we are aiming for here.

This sort of operation can be carried out any time between early summer, when new needles are hardening off, and early autumn. If you try this too late in the year the tiny wounds caused by severe bending of the branches will not have time to seal themselves against winter frosts and die-back may result.

You don't have to complete a task like this in one sitting, take several weeks over it if you like. In fact the tree will thank you if you do since a staged operation is less traumatic. Having completed the styling exercise wait until the following year before you repot. If by then the tree still seems weak wait another year. Check the wire regularly and replace it when it becomes too tight, coiling it in the opposite direction.

1 The raw material. It has plenty of branches plus a small, secondary trunk. The main trunk forks about halfway up, and the thickest fork is removed first.

2 Pines always produce whorls of branches like these. If allowed to remain they form thick 'knuckles' and disfigure the trunk. All but one or two branches must be pruned.

3 Most branches have been pruned, leaving only those which are needed for the design. The front, which displays the best trunk shape, is marked with a pencil stuck in the pot.

4 The secondary trunk is positioned so it is visible from the front. All old needles are removed to make wiring easier and to encourage back budding before wiring the lower left branch.

5 The main branches are positioned to cascade gently from the trunks, and curves are introduced to the upper trunk. The original leader is removed and replaced with a smaller branch.

Left: Stage one is complete. The pointed crown will be rounded off in time, and may even be lowered by pruning away the apex and replacing it with a lower branch. Branches will be periodically thinned back to new shoots sprouting from old wood.

6 Wires are not sufficient to hold the secondary trunk in place, so a tourniquet fixed to the pot's rim takes the strain. This can be tightened a little every few weeks if necessary.

7 Thick branches can be made to bend closer to the trunk by gently splitting them away from the trunk and using thick wire, or a stone, to hold the split open. The wound must be sealed.

8 These fine white strands are mycelium of a mycorrhyzal fungus which helps the tree absorb nutrients from the soil. If you find this in a pot, keep it. Root aphids look similar at first, but the insects are clearly visible.

9 After more thinning, the secondary branches are wired into position. The bonsai is now taking shape, but there is more to do. Every shoot must be wired to face outwards or upwards, to form domed pads.

8

AGING & REFINEMENT

Jins

One interpretation of the Japanese term *jin* is 'Godhead', but its definition in bonsai terms is rather less spiritual. Basically a jin is a dead branch which has shed its bark. In nature such branches are etched by the wind and rain and become bleached by the sun. They are frequently seen on most old conifers and even on some deciduous trees, notably oak.

By artificially creating jins on a bonsai you can impart a feeling of great age, and when done with care, their form and colour can complement the foliage masses to great effect. Get into the habit of creating jins every time you branch prune conifers, rather than removing the branch completely. If you don't like it after having lived with it for a while you can always cut it off later.

You can create jins at normal pruning time, but the best time is during the summer, when the bark is full of sap and is easier to strip and the wound will heal quickly.

Once you have made the jin you can give it texture by tearing the grain or by carving and sanding it to the desired shape. A jin will appear larger with a coarse texture than it would if given a smoother finish, so remember: the smaller the bonsai, the smoother the jin.

Another good point to bear in mind is that on a developing bonsai the foliage masses will grow, but the jins won't! If your new jins look too big now, they may well be in better proportion in a few year's time, so don't be too hasty in reducing their size at first.

This overgrown Chinese juniper resembles a bush rather than a dignified tree.

1 To create a jin, cut through the bark around the base of the branch. Then make another cut along its length. Make the cut 'eye-shaped' as marked in white.

2 Squeezing the bark with some flat-jawed pliers helps separate the bark from the wood. This is especially effective during spring and summer, when the sap is on the move.

3 The bark should peel away quite easily. If you are doing this in the autumn you may find the bark is a bit more stubborn, and you may need to scrape the wood clean.

4 A natural-looking shape and texture can be created by peeling back slivers of wood, exposing the grain. Jins look better if they are randomly formed rather than being carved.

1 Branches on vigorous trees tend to grow straight, whereas a curved jin may well be more appropriate. To bend a newly-formed jin, start by heating it gently with a low flame. Protect nearby foliage from the heat.

2 After a few minutes the heat will soften the resin, making the wood flexible. This enables you to bend the jin into the desired shape. Don't force the jin to bend before it is ready.

By creating jins out of selected branches we have increased the apparent age of the juniper and given it greater poise.

3 Hold the jin in the desired position until it has cooled completely. If you are not entirely happy with the result you can try again. The blackened wood bleaches easily with lime sulphur.

5 The shaped jin can be refined, and any fuzz can be removed, with fine sandpaper, or a piece of broken glass, although don't sand the jin perfectly smooth.

6 In nature jins are bleached by the sun. In bonsai this effect is achieved by treating them with lime sulphur, which also preserves the wood. Lime sulphur smells foul, so work outside.

Sharis

Sharis are related to jins but reflect a much more dramatic struggle with nature, causing a loss of bark from the trunk. This could be the result of lightning, disease, the battle with the elements, or it may just be the way the tree naturally ages.

Like jins, sharis are more appropriate on conifer bonsai, but for inspiration on deciduous trees take a look at our lowland pollarded willows with split trunks, or ancient hollow oaks.

The extreme use of sharis is employed in the creation of driftwood style bonsai. They are carved and refined to form wonderful shapes and textures which become more visually significant than the foliage masses. This is true living sculpture which, with the right balance of driftwood, tree and pot, represents the highest level of bonsai as an art form.

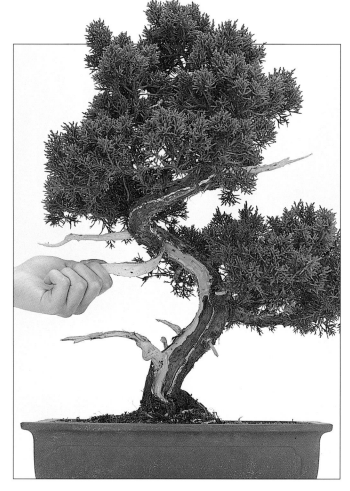

- It is best to take several seasons to create an extensive shari, stripping of a little more bark each time.

- Bark is part of the tree's transport system, so always leave enough to support the foliage. On no account remove bark from immediately below a branch or it will die.

- Never allow a shari to encircle the trunk completely or the tree will die above that point.

- Junipers will live happily with a spiral of living bark provided the shari is created gradually over several seasons. Pines will accept a gentle curve but spruces require a more or less straight line of living tissue from root to branch.

- Give the bonsai the proper aftercare by placing it in a lightly sheltered spot until all the remaining branches show new growth.

1 Mark the outline of the shari with white paint before you cut. Make the line of the shari echo the shape of the trunk. Cut through to the wood.

2 If you do this in summer, when the sap is flowing, the bark will come away cleanly. The dark area is where the exposed wood of the original shari has weathered.

3 Seal the edges of the shari with narrow strips of cut paste in order to prevent the cut surfaces from drying out.

- Lime sulphur does preserve the exposed wood as well as bleaching it, but one application lasts for only a short time. However, its effect is cumulative, so repeated twice-yearly applications will eventually almost 'fossilise' the wood.

- Very large areas of exposed wood may begin to decay at the base, where the trunk is constantly moist. These areas can be treated with clear horticultural preservative, a little at a time. *But don't let any run off into the soil.*

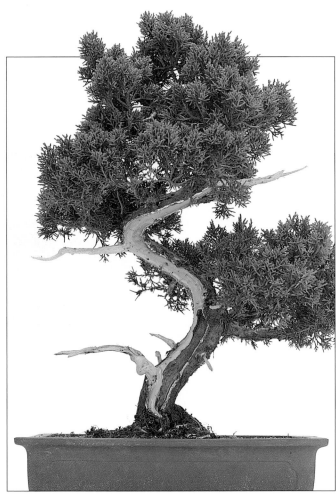

4 Note how the shari and jins flow from one another. Also, note how the shari runs from one side of the trunk to the other, enhancing the natural movement of the trunk line.

5 As with jins, the exposed wood must be treated with lime sulphur to preserve and bleach it. The old shari will blend with the new one after a couple of applications.

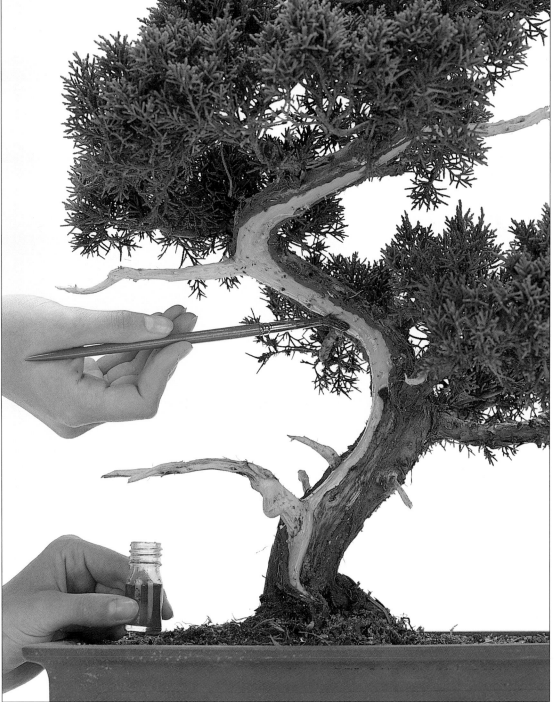

Refining the image

When fully refined and preened, ready for display, the bonsai image should appear almost as if it is frozen in time. Each branch should be perfectly positioned and clearly defined, with each neatly trimmed foliage pad floating in its own space.

As with all artistic disciplines, much depends on the aesthetic taste of the individual, but it is surprising how many experienced bonsai artists always seem to return to the classic Japanese principles, which have, after all, been developed over many years.

There is a grace and poise about classic Japanese bonsai, which can literally take your breath away. The ability to create a near-perfect image by using the minimum number of elements has taken many centuries to develop and refine, and will continue to set the standard for many years to come.

No bonsai is perfect, and the fact that all bonsai are living, growing plants means that they are constantly changing, and therefore require repeated attention to maintain their image. Even so, they can only look their absolute best for a few

The apex is still a little heavy and isolated from the rest of the tree. Lowering the lower left branchlets might solve both problems.

This foliage pad is too round and needs to be divided into two shallower pads.

There are too many small banches in this area. As the foliage fills out, some will be removed.

These long jins appear to be flung outwards by centrifugal force, giving energy to the design.

Introducing texture in the shari, by carving, would enhance its appearance.

The shari could be widened at the base to include part of the next root along. This would visually emphasise the root spread.

This delicate oval pot is more sympathetic than the original heavy, brown rectangle.

2 *Equally dramatic, this windswept style involves changing the planting angle, and using a slab instead of a pot. Some branches on the right are removed and the rest are re-aligned to the horizontal plane. The foliage pads become longer and shallower.*

1 *By removing all branches, except for the one just below the top curve of the trunk, a fine lierati style could is created. The shari has been extended and spiralled around the trunk, and a delicate, round pot is selected.*

This area is still a little heavy and needs to be thinned out and re-shaped.

These branches are a bit messy, but will appear less so once the foliage pads have filled out and are more clearly defined.

The shari could be extended around the back of the trunk, to re-appear on the inside of this curve.

Negative areas, or spaces between the foliage pads, make the tree look older.

Eventually, with constant pinching of new growth, all the foliage pads will be as cleanly defined as this one.

Although this branch lends stability to the design, it is too rigid and juvenile in form. The foliage pad should be encouraged to deepen until it conceals the branch.

This silly little jin should either be removed or drastically shortened

Left: *This is the tree used on pages 76 – 79. Every shoot has now been trimmed and wired into position. The wiring operation took a total of eighteen hours to complete.*

weeks at a time, after which they will, again, gradually begin to outgrow their ideal form.

This tree has had its image refined for the first time, but there are still many faults in the design. Over the next five or six years it will go through similar processes many more times, hopefully improving on each occasion. Eventually it may reach the stage where I am totally satisfied with it. In a way I hope this never happens, because then the challenge will end.

At some point in the distant future, a new owner may decide to change the front, or the planting angle. Perhaps the whole style may even be changed by removing and reshaping branches, or lowering the apex.

The comments and diagrams on these pages form a kind of critical analysis of the existing design, and offer some suggestions for alternative styles. Hopefully, these will help to guide your thoughts during those quiet moments of contemplation, when you and your tree plan your futures together.

3 The shohin bonsai below uses only the two lowest branches, which need several applications of wire before they can be positioned correctly. Splitting the thick branch from the trunk (see page 75) improves its angle. The top part of the trunk is split and bent using heat (see page 77). Tilting a little to the right creates a more dynamic image.

4 By turning the tree through 45 degrees anticlockwise, and removing the upper branches, a much more compact style evolves. The lower left branch has been brought round from the back, and all foliage pads widened. The apical jin is optional.

9

PROJECTS

Broom style zelkova

There is only one species which is eminently suitable for this style – the Japanese grey-barked elm, *zelkova serrata*, and it is no coincidence that it grows in this habit in nature. Other deciduous species can be used, but none perform as well.

The creation of such a geometric, uniform branch structure requires an equally precise and calculated approach, which is almost invariably successful. The only element of chance is in the placement of the new shoots as they emerge from the severed trunk. However, there are normally so many that you would be very unlucky not to get off to a good start.

The plant you select must have a trunk thickness anything from three-quarters of an inch to four inches or more. If the trunk is too thin it will be impossible to execute the initial cut accurately and it is more likely to throw out shoots from lower down rather than from the cambium layer exposed by the cut.

Once the sequence illustrated has been followed, adopt an annual regime of allowing shoots to grow four or five leaves and then trimming back to two. A vigorous, well fed tree may require this treatment several times during each growing season. Prune out crossing branches in late winter. Gradually you will build up a network of evenly spaced branches with ever-decreasing internodes.

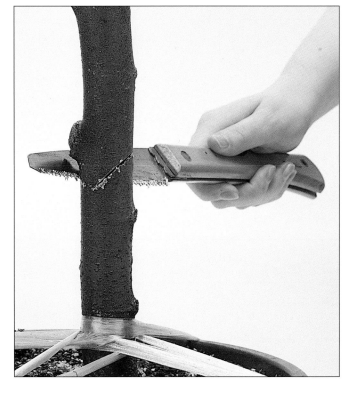

1 *Before you start, make sure the plant is in good health and is firmly tied into its container. This will help prevent too much strain on the roots during cutting. The best time for this technique is early spring, before the production of new foliage has used up any of the tree's stored energy.*

2 *Decide how tall you want the trunk to be – the ideal proportion is about four times its width. Using a very sharp, fine-toothed saw, make two cuts which form an unequal sided, 'V'-shaped surface.*

3 *Clean up any ragged edges with a sharp knife and seal the entire cut surface, especially around the edge, where the cambium layer is located.*

4 *Within six or seven weeks new shoots should push through the sealant. Sometimes these shoots take longer to appear, so be patient.*

5 *Tie some waterproof tape tightly around the emerging shoots. This ensures a smooth transition from trunk to branch without unsightly swelling.*

6 The new shoots will grow rapidly. By the time they have reached this size they will have hardened off and will be ready for a prune.

Regular pruning over many years is responsible for this uniform branch structure.

7 The long shoots are all cut back to two or three leaves. You may need to thin out some of the weaker shoots as well.

The pattern of the branches is reflected in the surface root formation.

Above: A classic broom style, or hokidachi, zelkova. It would have taken up to ten years or more to develop this fine tracery of twigs.

8 New shoots will grow from each leaf axil, and they, too, will be shortened. This cycle will need to be repeated many times over.

Informal upright maple

Once a young tree has been allowed to thicken to about half an inch or so it becomes virtually impossible to bend. What's more, if allowed to grow freely it will lack taper and thus become useless as it is for bonsai purposes. However, you can still take advantage of the tree's natural resilience to create an informal upright style with severe taper, by employing this 'prune-and-grow' technique.

Any deciduous species can be used but Japanese maples are by far the most successful. The fact that they have opposite leaves, and therefore produce new shoots opposite each other, creates a mechanical growth pattern. This enables you to position the branches exactly on the outside of bends in the trunk – which is aesthetically more pleasing – and also means that the branch structure will echo the trunk's angular form.

The tree we have chosen here is five years old and has been grown in open ground for the past three years. In common with most trees of this age, it has retained two small, weak branches which mark the position of the end of the first season's growth. These will be developed to become the new leader and the first major branch.

If these branches are not present you will still be able to detect the 'eyes' or locations of the dormant buds from which such branches will grow. The initial cut should be made in precisely the same way as illustrated, and within a few weeks the new shoots will emerge. This operation should be carried out in early spring, before the buds have opened.

This process of allowing extension growth and pruning back to suitably positioned shoots or nodes should be repeated another two to four times – no more – before the final height is attained. A tree with too many sharp bends in a tall trunk looks unnatural.

1 The roots of this newly-dug Japanese maple are wrapped to preserve moisture while the trunk is cut directly above the bottom two branches or dormant buds.

2 The branch on the left is chosen to become the new leader and is pruned at the point where the next angle is planned, just above a pair of buds. The large wound must be sealed.

3 Select a large clay pot to encourage rapid growth and development. The long roots should be shortened to promote a compact root structure. Water and feed well.

4 Plant the tree at an angle so that one branch is horizontal, and the other – the new leader – points upwards at a similar angle to the trunk, but in the opposite direction.

7 *Two shoots are left to become the second branch and the new leader. This time another shoot is also left at the rear to form the first back branch.*

8 *Another few weeks pass and the maple is ready for its third prune of the season. Free draining soil with frequent watering and feeding produces this vigorous growth, essential for rapid trunk development .*

5 *After a few weeks of vigorous growth, encouraged by heavy feeding, a mass of new shoots will have appeared. The first cycle is complete and it is time for more pruning.*

9 *The third pruning leaves three side branches, one to the rear, and four sections of trunk. One more year and the structure will be complete.*

6 *Maples produce a lot of small shoots around pruning scars. These should be thinned out so all the tree's energy is concentrated in the developing trunk.*

Beech group

Most species can be used for creating bonsai groups and the results can be almost instantly satisfying. The main effect is achieved by the interplay between the trunks of different thicknesses and lines, and the actual branch structure is less important than it is with a single tree. Successful groups can be created from young, spindly plants which would normally be little or no use as single trees, so this is a good way to utilise seedlings or cuttings which you would otherwise discard.

We have chosen some rooted beech cuttings which were intended for hedging. This type of raw material is usually sold in large numbers, so it is very cheap, and there is always plenty to choose from. Other hedging stock includes hawthorn, elm, privet, field maple etc.

It is important to select plants of different heights and thicknesses in order to create perspective and interest. Stick to odd numbers, they are easier to compose (the Japanese actually have a superstitious aversion to even numbers) and avoid the temptation to use too many plants at first. A group of more than nine or so becomes a forest, which is subject to slightly different aesthetic principles.

Create your group in early spring, and keep it in a humid and well ventilated place, such as an open-ended polytunnel, until the roots are established and growth is evident. Little or no wiring should be necessary since the foliage will hide the branches and will merely act as a visual foil to the trunk arrangement. Any branches growing towards the centre of the group should be removed and from then on all you will need to do is prune new growth and thin out cluttered shoots.

4 The clay balls keep the trees in position while they are being arranged in the pot. Start with the tallest tree, just off centre, and place the two next tallest either side.

1 These beech cuttings are not particularly inspiring at first sight, but their different thicknesses and lines are just what we need to create a group.

2 Cut away the long roots with sharp scissors, leaving as many fine feeder roots as possible.

3 Work a sticky mixture of equal parts of clay and fine peat between the roots, and mould them into a ball.

5 Build up the design tree by tree, adding the smaller ones at the sides and rear to create perspective. Leaning the trees away from the centre gives the illusion of greater size.

6 When the arrangement is complete add soil between the clay balls. Dry soil is easier to apply as it does not stick to the wet clay.

9 The new planting is already pleasing to the eye. Note how the trees at the edges have been pruned so each apex sweeps outwards.

In nature, small trees at the edge of a group will naturally grow out towards the light.

7 Carefully work the soil into all the spaces between the rootballs using a pencil (or chopstick if you want to be authentic). Ensure that all the spaces are filled with soil.

Crossing branches and those growing towards the centre of the composition have been removed.

It is important not to allow any trunk to obscure another.

8 You can complete the picture by 'landscaping' the soil surface with different kinds of moss and grit. Water the pot and moss thoroughly first, and avoid pressing the moss down too hard.

Varying the spaces between the trees produces a more natural effect.

Forest on a slab

Most species capable of producing relatively tall, slender trunks can be used for forest plantings, but you should avoid those which produce a proliferation of back buds, such as cotoneaster or Chinese elm. These will soon become congested and will be a nightmare to keep thinned out. Pines are seldom used in large numbers since they are prone to disease when overcrowded, but most other conifers are eminently suitable.

The most important thing to remember when planting a forest is that it should have depth and perspective as well as width. Although the actual front-to-back depth of the pot – or more often slab – may be only a foot or so you have to create the illusion of several hundred yards at least and hint at an almost infinite unseen depth. There are a few simple rules which, if followed, will guarantee a successful planting.

• Select plants of different heights and thicknesses.

• Width is achieved by planting the largest trees towards the centre and front and reducing the heights progressively at either side and behind, leaning the end few outwards slightly.

• Perspective is achieved by planting the smallest trees at the back and leaning them away from the viewer.

• A few smaller trees planted in front will look younger rather than further away. The fact that the eye has to travel beyond these to the larger trees creates the illusion of depth in the composition.

• No three trees should be in a straight line when viewed from *any* angle.

• When viewed from the front, no trunk should be obscured by another.

• The trunks of the tallest trees should be free of branches until they are clear of the smaller trees at the front and rear, thus allowing the eye unimpeded access to the whole forest.

1 The first step is to choose your stone slab, which should ideally have an irregular, narrow shape. This one is a piece of slate from Devon, bought from a local garden centre. It is about three feet long and quite heavy.

Below: This newly created forest already has a realistic appearance. As with smaller groups, care must be taken to avoid overlapping the trunks and to vary the spaces between them.

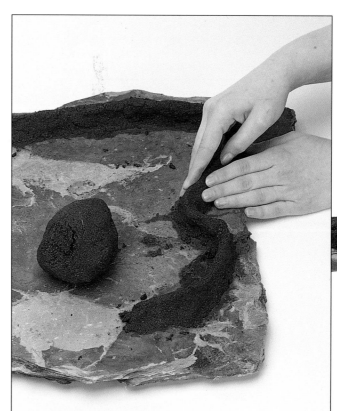

2 Build a low wall with a sticky mix of clay and fine peat to stop the soil washing off the slab.

3 Leave a generous margin around the wall and fill the inside with a one-inch layer of soil.

88

4 *Choose young plants of different sizes. We are using one to three-year-old larch seedlings.*

5 *Forest trees have tall, clean trunks, so you will need to trim off all the lower branches. Leaving a few low branches on some of the smaller trees will make them look younger, adding realism to the composition.*

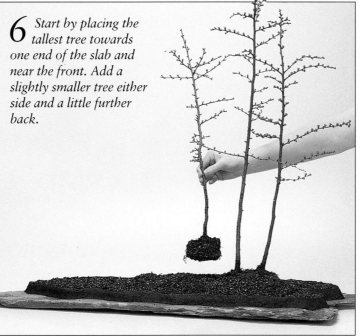

6 *Start by placing the tallest tree towards one end of the slab and near the front. Add a slightly smaller tree either side and a little further back.*

7 *Repeat the last step towards the other end, using slightly smaller trees.*

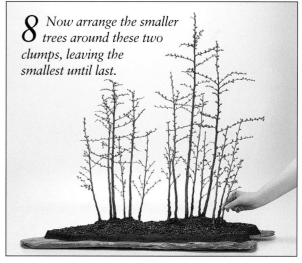

8 *Now arrange the smaller trees around these two clumps, leaving the smallest until last.*

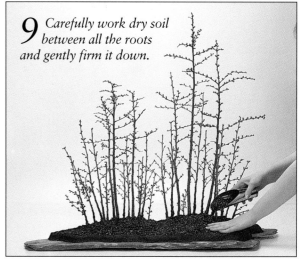

9 *Carefully work dry soil between all the roots and gently firm it down.*

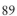

Raft planting

This raft style needle juniper is very old, and has developed into a classic bonsai. The tallest trunk is nearly three feet high.

'Plant a tree and let it grow. Let that tree set seed and after five hundred years you may have a forest.'

There are, however, quicker and more efficient ways to create realistic forests in miniature, and the raft technique is the most reliable of all.

It has one major advantage over the traditional method of using individual trees of different ages. This is simply that each 'tree' doesn't have to compete with its neighbours for food and water, so there is little risk of the smaller and weaker ones dying off. It also means that each individual 'tree' is identical in colour and vigour.

The process is simple and can be successfully applied to any species. All you need is a plant with as many branches as possible of different thicknesses and lengths all tending to grow from one side of the trunk. It will help with the design if the plant also has some very low branches as you will see.

With Blaauws juniper you can carry out this operation at any time between February and June, but with other species early spring is best. After a year or two the new roots will be able to support the tree on their own and the original root mass can be cut off.

You can still see the original trunk just below the soil surface.

1 *Blaauws junipers (juniperus media blaauwii) like this are common in all garden centres, and are quite inexpensive.*

2 *Lay the plant on its side and wire-train all the branches upwards. Try to spread them as you go to give a three-dimensional effect, and bring the lower branches back towards the roots.*

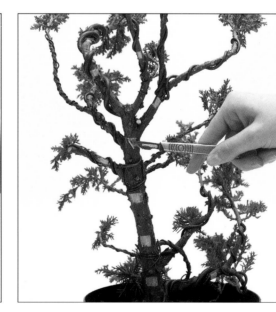

3 *Cut out some sections of bark on the underside of the trunk. New roots will form around the wounds, which will sustain the tree when the original roots are eventually removed.*

Note how the trunks
fan out from the base.

4 *Carefully comb out the roots,*
especially on the underside of the
root ball, taking care not to cause
unnecessary damage. Any heavy roots
which grow upwards can be cut off.

5 *Gently fold the roots underneath the*
trunk and lay the whole thing flat on a
one-inch bed of bonsai soil in a suitable
shallow container. Spread the roots out
over the soil.

6 *New roots will not form along the*
trunk unless it is covered with soil.
Wire is passed through the drainage
holes to hold the trunk down
firmly.

7 *Mound more soil over the*
trunk and roots. Work it
between the branches.

8 *Moss and grit can be*
added to create a
realistic effect. Once the
new planting has grown a
little the trunks and
branches can be properly
wire-trained.

Shohin, exposed root style

This dwarf spruce (*Picea 'little gem'*) is very easy to work with. The growth is so profuse and compact that you can style the basic bonsai shape with very little wiring. It tolerates root pruning well and readily produces back budding. It is a perfect species for creating *shohin* or miniature bonsai. (The phrase 'shohin' literally translates as 'small goods'). There is no official size restriction for shohin but they are generally no taller six or seven inches. The Japanese say 'feel' is more important than size.

Shohin bonsai need more careful watering since they both dry out and become waterlogged quicker than larger trees. Keep them in the shade during the hottest part of the day, and their roots need severe frost protection during winter (*see page 108*).

Hidden treasure
One of the exciting things about this type of raw material is that you never quite know what you have got until you actually start work. In this case the initial inspection of the roots, in order to find the best viewing angle, revealed a mass of fairly thick roots growing like a spider's legs from one side of the trunk's base. The original intention was to create an informal upright or semi-cascade style, but these roots are too good to hide so neagari it is!

1 Dense foliage and a root ball to match mean that this little spruce can be worked on at any time during spring and early summer.

2 The first step is to clear away all the debris and fine shoots from the trunk and heavier branches, so you can see the internal branch structure more clearly.

3 Next, some of the low branches are pruned away to leave a clearly defined trunk. Too many branches will make the bonsai look juvenile and will prevent light reaching the inner foliage.

4 Potting the tree at this stage will help you to judge the proportions more easily. However, the tree needs to be tied tightly into the pot to avoid further damage to the roots.

5 Further trimming is again needed. This time to remove more unwanted branches and to clean fine growth from the bases of the remaining branches.

6 The only wiring necessary in this case is on the major branches, which need to be brought down to a horizontal plane, thus imparting the illusion of age.

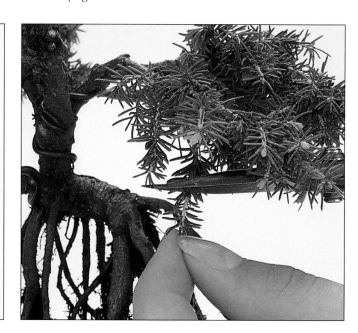

Above *Only basic wiring was necessary to style this tree. In time new buds will form along the tops of the foliage pads, giving them a domed outline. These will need to be thinned out periodically.*

7 The crown of any tree is more vigorous than the lower parts, so this needs extra thinning to prevent it from using up too much growth energy, and to improve appearance.

8 Finally, any fine, exposed hair roots should be cut away, as they are likely to whither anyway. Shoots which grow down from the foliage pads also need to be trimmed off.

Root over rock

One of the most dramatic of all bonsai styles echoes a tree's struggle for survival in the harsh terrain of the mountains, where the roots have had to weave their way between the rocks in search of water and nutrients. Over the years the scarce soil becomes eroded to expose the root formation clinging tightly to the host rock. In bonsai, as in nature, this process takes many years to complete, but if done with skill and care the result is well worth waiting for.

It is essential to take your time in selecting the right materials for your creation. The rock should be stable enough not to flake away in time, so avoid soft slate, chalk or crumbly sandstone. It should also have lots of fissures and cracks to accommodate the roots. The texture should be fine enough to give the impression of a larger rock, in scale with the tree.

Virtually any species of tree or shrub can be used but quicker results are achieved with fast-growing varieties which naturally have thick, fleshy roots, such as maples, elms, larch etc. Pines and junipers take longer to establish on the rock although the finished product can be stunning. You should avoid plants whose roots are slow to thicken, such as cotoneaster and azalea.

You can use a deep container as shown here or, better still, plant the assembly in open ground and leave it to grow undisturbed for at least three years. An occasional dose of a high phosphate fertiliser will promote thicker roots.

After the first three years the plant can be lifted and the roots which grow beyond the base of the rock can be trimmed back. It should then be replanted in a deep container. Each year from now on, at repotting time, you can remove some of the surface soil, gradually exposing the roots. At the same time you should raise the rock a little in the container. Don't rush this process. Remember that roots thicken much faster below ground than when exposed to the air – the longer you wait, the better the result.

During this period you can train the trunk and branches, bearing in mind that the more you restrict the top growth the slower the roots will develop.

The exact length of time this process will take depends largely on the size and species, but with luck, after seven or eight years, this unsightly object can be planted in a suitable pot and will suddenly become a majestic and exciting bonsai.

3 You may need to try several plants before you find one with suitable roots. This Chinese elm does the trick.

4 Position the tree comfortably on the side of the rock, A tree perched on top of a rock looks awkward. Press the roots into the clay-filled fissures.

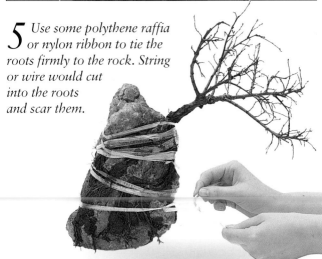

5 Use some polythene raffia or nylon ribbon to tie the roots firmly to the rock. String or wire would cut into the roots and scar them.

1 This piece of water-worn limestone is ideal for root over rock style bonsai. It has plenty of fissures and looks very old.

2 Mix some moist clay and fine peat to the consistency of modelling clay and press it into the fissures. This will give the roots a medium to grow through.

6 Next, wrap the rock in polythene and secure it. This forces the roots to grow downwards, following the lines of the fissures.

7 If you are using a container, only fill about a third of it with soil to start with, so that all the roots can be buried.

8 The top few inches can be filled with gravel to stop the roots growing upwards. When watering, allow some to run down inside the polythene.

Below: *Trident maple are excellent subjects for root over rock bonsai. This four foot giant weighs several hundred-weight. The shape of the tree blends perfectly with that of the rock.*

This is in fact two trees which have become fused together. Their leaves emerge in slightly different colours in spring.

Note how the roots follow the natural sweep of the rock.

The Japanese Ibigawa rock has all the character of a rugged mountain.

Wrap-arounds

Here we attach living plants to driftwood, in order to create a single unit. You can produce a fair driftwood style bonsai out of otherwise useless material. Traditionalists despise bonsai created in this manner. The Japanese call them *'Tanuki'*, or cheats, after the legendary bear who could not be trusted.

The driftwood should be sound and preserved with colourless horticultural preservative several months before you attach the plant. The label on the preservative can must say: 'Harmless to plants once solvent has evaporated' or something very similar.

If the driftwood has an unstable base you can bed it in a pad of glass-fibre resin, cement or car filler paste, leaving space for the trunk and roots of the plants to fit closely to the wood. Make sure the pad will not obscure any future drainage holes.

The plants will be undergoing considerable surgery so they need to be healthy and vigorous. Trunks must be thick enough to survive being split or shaved, half an inch at the very least, but not so thick that it cannot blend with the contours of the driftwood. Because this technique also involves root disturbance it is best to do it in late spring.

It will take anything from four to ten years of vigorous growth for the living trunk to spread and become firmly attached to the driftwood. During this time you should replace the raffia or tape annually to avoid scarring the bark. Avoid the temptation to see how it's doing by trying to pick it away from the driftwood. If it comes away now you will have to start all over again!

NB. Never use ferrous metal on junipers. A reaction between the metal and the sap causes decay around the wound. This reaction spreads and rapidly kills the tree.

Above: This very old driftwood style needle juniper is the genuine article, but it gives you a good idea of the kind of image you can create given enough time.

1 The raw materials. The driftwood is the remains of an old christmas tree which has been treated with preservative (see text). The plants are Blaauws junipers.

2 First split or shave the trunk to form a flat surface which fits flush to the driftwood. This calls for strong nerves, a sharp, sturdy knife and a steady hand.

3 Test the progress of the work as you go, and make adjustments as necessary. It is important that the cut surface fits the driftwood closely.

4 Temporarily attach the plant in position with wire, and drill pilot holes through the trunk and into the driftwood, every two or three inches.

5 Now firmly fix the plant to the driftwood using solid brass screws, **never** steel or plated screws. Don't let the screwdriver slip, or you may cause serious damage to the remaining bark.

6 Drive the screws through the bark to hold the plant firm. The heads will heal over in a year or two. You may need to carve the driftwood to ensure a good fit.

7 Next, bind the plant tightly with waterproof tape. I use nylon taffeta – it is strong and does not rot. This encourages the trunk to spread sideways as it grows, so it will grip the driftwood more effectively.

8 Plant the tree in a large pot to encourage rapid growth and development. It is best to do this work in spring, so the plants can begin to recover straight away, and have a full growing season ahead.

97

Thread grafting

This is the only type of grafting I would recommend for the amateur. For some reason it is seldom used in conventional horticulture, which is surprising because it is so easy to do and nearly always works.

Its most simple application is in creating new branches to improve a bonsai's design. If you are really ambitious you can graft an entire branch structure of a variety with, say, attractive leaves or flowers onto a more interesting trunk of a different variety which does not have these desirable characteristics. Needless to say, both branches and trunk must be of the same species.

The tree shown here has a fairly interesting trunk and root spread but has no branches at all until the very top. So we will use the thread grafting technique to create new branches exactly where we want them. The tree has been prepared by allowing a good supply of long supple shoots to grow.

1 Test the shoots you want to use for the thread graft to make sure they are long enough and supple enough to be positioned accurately without snapping.

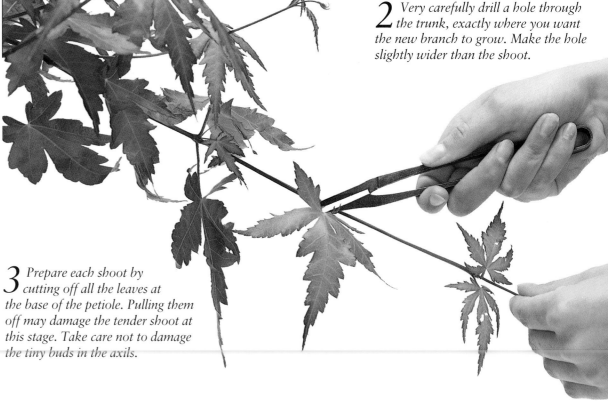

2 Very carefully drill a hole through the trunk, exactly where you want the new branch to grow. Make the hole slightly wider than the shoot.

3 Prepare each shoot by cutting off all the leaves at the base of the petiole. Pulling them off may damage the tender shoot at this stage. Take care not to damage the tiny buds in the axils.

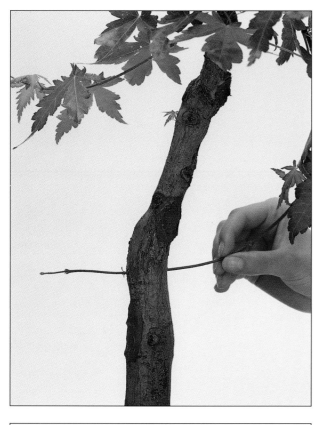

4 *Thread the shoot through the hole in the trunk until it is a tight fit, or as far as it will go without snapping. Take care not to knock off any buds.*

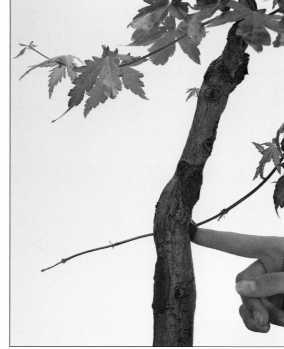

5 *Seal the hole either side of the trunk to prevent moisture loss, which would cause the edges of the wound to recede, taking longer to heal.*

6 *You can graft on as many branches as you like in one session. As the wound heals over and the shoot naturally thickens, the two cambium layers are forced together, causing the graft union.*

7 *After several month's vigorous growth the shoot is thicker where it exits the trunk than where it enters, indicating that the graft has taken.*

8 *When you are sure the graft has been successful you can sever each shoot where it enters the trunk and seal all the cuts. Protect the tree from strong sun and spray it daily for a few weeks.*

THREAD GRAFTING ROOTS

You can use the same technique to graft on new roots. The hole is drilled at the base of the trunk and the stem of a healthy seedling or rooted cutting is passed through it. The roots of the seedling are planted in the host tree's container. Once the graft has taken the top portion of the stem is cut away, and the lower part becomes a new surface root. The root to the right of the picture was grafted in this way.

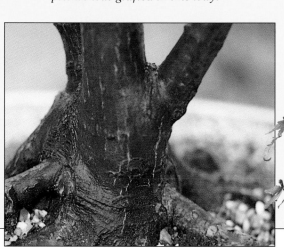

Watering and feeding

Watering

In theory, provided your bonsai is growing in a free-draining soil *(see page 36)*, it should not be possible to over water. But many beginners, in their enthusiasm, manage to do just that. Over watering eliminates the air contained in the spaces between the soil particles and 'drowns' the roots. It also creates the conditions favoured by various root-rotting fungi. The symptoms of decaying roots (yellowing foliage and lack of new growth) are not usually apparent until the damage has already been done. Having said this, it does take a few weeks for the problem to become serious, so the odd drenching now and then won't hurt. On the other hand it may only take twenty-four hours for a bonsai to die of thirst, so it is essential to prevent the soil drying out completely.

Generally the best method is to water the surface of the soil evenly, using a fine rose or spray, until the water drains out of the drainage holes. Wait a few minutes and repeat. This ensures a thorough wetting of the soil and should be sufficient for one day during the height of summer. Try to avoid watering a tree that doesn't really need it. Wind can dry the soil's surface to a crisp, while deeper in the pot it may still be quite wet. If in doubt check by scraping away the surface in a couple of places and adjust the amount of water accordingly.

The best time to water is in early evening. This gives the tree plenty of time to have a good drink before morning. If you water in the morning the tree doesn't have much of a chance to refresh itself before the heat of the day. If you can't avoid watering in the morning do it as early as possible. Another advantage with evening watering is that you can douse the foliage at the same time without the risk of

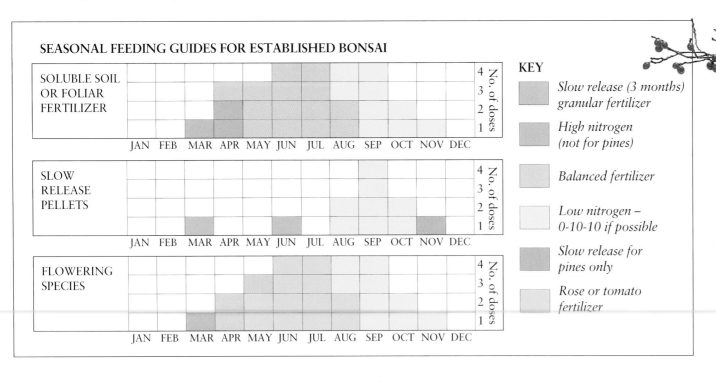

SEASONAL FEEDING GUIDES FOR ESTABLISHED BONSAI

SOLUBLE SOIL OR FOLIAR FERTILIZER — No. of doses (1–4) — JAN FEB MAR APR MAY JUN JUL AUG SEP OCT NOV DEC

SLOW RELEASE PELLETS — No. of doses (1–4) — JAN FEB MAR APR MAY JUN JUL AUG SEP OCT NOV DEC

FLOWERING SPECIES — No. of doses (1–4) — JAN FEB MAR APR MAY JUN JUL AUG SEP OCT NOV DEC

KEY

Slow release (3 months) granular fertilizer

High nitrogen (not for pines)

Balanced fertilizer

Low nitrogen – 0-10-10 if possible

Slow release for pines only

Rose or tomato fertilizer

leaf scorch caused by the water droplets acting as miniature magnifying glasses in the sun. All bonsai appreciate a daily shower.

A word of warning. Don't assume that the rain will do the watering for you. A bonsai acts like an umbrella, and it shelters the pot from all but the heaviest downpour. Your neighbours might think you're crazy, but it is well worth continuing to check the need to water even in wet weather.

Feeding

This can be a source of much confusion for the novice but the principle is really quite simple. There are three ways to apply fertiliser: by placing pellets on or in the soil, by watering it onto the soil and by spraying it on the leaves (foliar feeding). Each has its own pros and cons and the choice is really based on your own preference.

Fertiliser pellets

Specialist bonsai fertiliser pellets are available from all nurseries. They can be either the organic variety such as rape seed cake, or inorganic. The inorganic pellets are coated in a porous membrane which allows the nutrient to pass by the process of osmosis. Both types release nutrients slowly, which means that you don't have to worry about feeding for a while. The disadvantage is that you won't be able to adjust the feeding pattern without risking over feeding, which may 'burn' the roots *(see page 16).*

Soil application

There are a large number of soluble fertilisers available in garden centres and florists, most of which are suitable. (Avoid using any specifically intended for house plants as they tend to be too rich for trees). These can be routinely applied once a week or, better still, at a quarter strength with every watering. *Never use a stronger solution than the manufacturers state.* It is a good idea to change brand every now and then, in order to maintain a balanced diet. The disadvantage here is that the nutrients wash out of the soil quickly, so you have to be quite strict in your feeding regime. Also, during prolonged spells of very wet weather you may not be able to feed your trees since they may not need any water.

Foliar feeding

Research has shown that a plant can absorb more nutrients through its leaves than through its roots. Many standard soluble fertilisers can be applied in this way as well as via the soil, while some are specifically designed to be applied in this manner. This technique is particularly useful when your bonsai has root problems or when the soil is constantly wet through heavy rain. Foliar feeds are easy to apply provided you don't do so in strong sun, otherwise the leaves may scorch. The only disadvantage is that in warm, windy weather the solution dries on the leaves too quickly and leaves a powdery deposit which is difficult to wash off.

Any of these methods of feeding are suitable for keeping an established tree in good health and vigour, but occasionally you may need to use a specialist feed in order to encourage the tree to perform in a specific way. Before you attempt this you will need to understand a little more about how each of the major nutrients affects the tree.

NPK?

These letters appear on the packs of all good fertilisers and are followed by a sequence of numbers, for example NPK 7 : 11 : 9.5. The letters are the chemical symbols for the three major nutrients and the numbers denote their ratio. The higher the numbers, the stronger the fertiliser. For bonsai it is wisest to stick with brands with weaker concentrations.

So our example has seven parts of nitrogen (N), eleven parts of phosphorus (P) and nine-and-a-half parts of potassium (K). It is a fairly well-balanced feed for sustaining growth. But what do each of these elements actually do?

This unusual and desirable clump style bonsai is Japanese holly, or Ilex serrata. (The Japanese call it English holly!) It is encouraged to flower and fruit prolifically by a high potassium diet.

Nitrogen

This is responsible for leaf and stem growth and can enrich the colour of the foliage. Without any nitrogen a plant would only produce a few stunted leaves and growth would be poor. The plant's health would quickly deteriorate because it would not be able to carry out the process of photosynthesis efficiently. Too much nitrogen and the growth will be too vigorous. Large leaves will be borne on long, sappy shoots which will soon outgrow their own strength, and the tree will be prone to disease.

Phosphorus

This is primarily responsible for root growth. It also encourages thick, sturdy trunks, helps to strengthen the plant against disease and frosts, and promotes back-budding. An excess may result in poor foliage growth and colour.

Potassium

Potassium, or potash, is responsible for encouraging flowers and fruit as well as hardening off late growth before the winter. If left out of its diet, a plant will fail to flower, or if it does then the blooms will be of poor quality and the fruit will not set. Potassium also helps to build up the plant's resistance to disease.

Special feeding programmes

From what we have learned above it is easy to deduce how we can use each element to produce specific results by increasing its proportion in the fertiliser. Here are some pointers as to why and when this should be done.

- *Nitrogen (N)* should be increased when you want a plant to put on a spurt of rapid growth. This applies to young, developing plants which you want to grow larger before starting to train. If the foliage is dull (not yellow – which indicates a root problem) a little extra nitrogen may improve the colour.

A high nitrogen feed should be applied as the tree needs it, not before. So in spring, *after* growth has started, or once new leaves have emerged following leaf pruning, an application of a high nitrogen feed will replenish the tree's resources.

- *Phosphorus (P)* is especially useful after repotting or when a tree is recovering from a root problem, so a little extra can be given at such times. In fact, a high phosphorus and potassium feed will aid recovery from many ailments.

Increasing the phosphorus content in the diet in late summer and autumn toughens up the tree in readiness for autumn. A pinch of powdered superphosphate on the surface of the soil is an easy method of application.

- *Potassium (K)* should be increased for all flowering and fruiting bonsai. A diluted rose or tomato feed is ideal, as these are specifically formulated to increase the flowering and fruiting potential. Potash can also be increased to help weak plants regain strength.

Extra potassium given during late summer and autumn will help the tree combat the perils of winter. A little sulphate of potash sprinkled on the soil once a week will do the trick.

Some nurseries sell a specialist soluble fertiliser called '0-10-10' which, as the name implies, is nitrogen free and is ideal for late season feeding. When buying fertilisers make sure that they include trace elements. These are only required in minute quantities but without them your bonsai will surely suffer. If you decide to use products which do not contain trace elements you should add them separately twice a year. There are various compounds available but you may need to search for them.

The chart on page 100 shows the ideal feeding programme which will provide your bonsai with all its dietary needs and keep it in good health.

Korean hornbeams naturally develop this attractive streaky bark, even in young trees.

A spacing bar is used to hold two trunks apart until they are set in the desired position.

Left: *The trunk lines of Korean hornbeams (Carpinus turczaninowii) make them ideal for group plantings. Foliar feeding is necessary to ensure that the smaller trees receive their fair share of nourishment.*

1 Organic fertiliser pellets can be either evenly distributed on the surface, or lightly pressed into the soil. They break down with watering and release the nutrients gradually over a three month period.

This wavy trunk line results from hard pruning the stem of a plant with alternate leaves.

2 Foliar feed can be applied either with a hand spray or a watering can. A spray allows localised feeding of weaker branches, in order to build up their strength.

Siting your bonsai

The choice of site for your bonsai display will depend largely on the layout of your garden, but it is important to consider your bonsai's requirements as well. Although different species prefer different conditions, it will help if you can keep all your collection in the same part of the garden in order to make daily watering and inspection a lot easier.

Conifers generally love to be in full sun all day and can even tolerate the heating of the pot and soil. Some tough deciduous species, such as elm, birch and hawthorn, also enjoy the sun but prefer their roots to be kept cooler. This can be achieved by placing them so that their pots are shaded from the afternoon sun by other trees.

Species with more delicate foliage, like Japanese maples, hornbeam and beech need to be protected from strong winds as well as sun. Azaleas also suffer from over-exposure to wind and sun. However, this does not mean that they should be placed in total shade.

Morning and evening sun can do no harm, but during the middle of the day they should be in the shadow of a nearby building or full-grown tree. Failing this, you can construct a canopy of greenhouse shading mesh which will simulate the dappled shade of the woodland margin where these plants naturally thrive.

Bonsai growing in small pots will all need a certain amount of shade, regardless of the species. Small pots heat up quickly, cooking the roots and drying the soil. A permanent shadery featuring a slatted roof eliminating fifty percent of the sunlight is ideal.

If you can't arrange this then put your trees against a west-facing wall, but remember to turn them round at regular intervals. Otherwise the branches at the rear will slow down and may eventually die.

Keep all bonsai on tables or custom-built benches – *never* on the ground. Every pest known to the gardener: slugs, ants, cats and even kids will conspire to destroy your collection in no time. Besides this, when your trees are displayed at eye-level you can appreciate them much more and will be able to spot pests and diseases a lot sooner. Benches should have slatted surfaces to allow air to circulate around the trees and the water to drain away.

Leave plenty of space between the trees so the lower branches receive light and air. Move them around occasionally so each side of the trees receive their fair share of sun. Large bonsai can be stood on 'monkey poles' – stout wooden posts with a platform firmly fixed to the top.

If you decide to go the whole way and construct a Japanese-style bonsai garden, keep it simple. Avoid the temptation to include too many lanterns, pagodas, stone buddhas and other Oriental 'garden gnomes'. The inclusion of some low-growing, lush plants like hostas and dwarf bamboo can help retain local humidity which will benefit the bonsai.

1 The insulated polycarbonate wall of a greenhouse makes an ideal backdrop for bonsai, as this one at Herons Nursery. Note how the suiseki (viewing stones) add interest.

2 Wooden trellis is less effective as a backdrop, but does provide dappled shade. The smaller trees are protected from the strong sun by the larger ones.

Right: *This is my own back yard. The shadery filters the sun during the afternoon, while the bigger trees on benches receive full sun all day. In really wet weather I drape a plastic sheet over the shadery to prevent waterlogging of the pots.*
Most of the materials are second-hand, the most expensive items being the pierced bricks supporting the benches.

3 *Displays which are open to the public need to be protected from curious visitors by a discreet rail. Paving slabs set in coarse gravel guide the viewer along the display. Two trees are temporarily placed on the gravel, in the shade of a cedar tree, while they recover from repotting.*

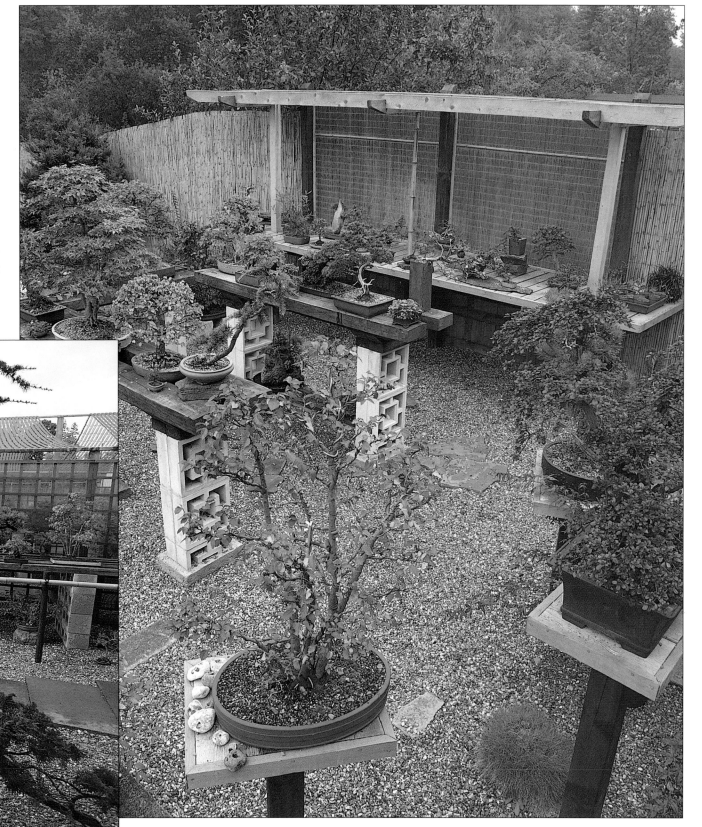

Preparing for a display

When bonsai are in a public show they come under very close scrutiny. It is essential that when your works of art are displayed they look their best. They should be sparkling with health and spotlessly clean.

All debris such as dead or discoloured leaves must be removed, and the surface of the soil must be free of weeds. The trunk and main branches will probably need cleaning, as will the pot.

It is very tempting to use bamboo or split cane as a backdrop to a display, but this is far too 'busy' and detracts attention from the trees. It is far better to use a pale, neutral coloured, untextured surface.

The same goes for the table, although woven reed matting can be used provided the trees are displayed on simple, low wooden stands. If you don't have suitable stands you can construct some low boxes and paint them the same colour as the backdrop. The important thing is to keep it simple.

Keep labels small and the information basic. You only need to state the species (botanical and common names), the style and the age. The owner's or artist's name can also be included.

Also, remember that the public will love to touch your bonsai, so take whatever precautions you can to prevent this happening. It is not unknown for people to try to take cuttings from bonsai displays!

2 Pick out all weeds and dead moss, making sure to pull out all the roots as well. This is good general practice anyway, even if you are not exhibiting the tree.

1 Sudy the outline of the tree carefully and snip off anything which breaks the periphery. A photograph often reveals faults the eye misses.

4 Juniper trunks should have all the flaky bark brushed off with an old toothbrush. Stubborn bits of bark in awkward places can be rubbed off with sandpaper.

*5 Once the bark has been removed, the trunk can be given added colour by burnishing it with a soft, lint-free cloth, moistened with **just a little** vegetable oil.*

3 *You can make the surface more attractive by dressing it with fresh soil. Standard soil with extra grit looks good, but fresh grit alone is too clean and looks out of place.*

6 *Deciduous trees tend to accumulate green algae on their trunks and branches. Although some people like green trunks, algae should always be scrubbed off before exhibiting.*

8 *Additional patina can be given to unglazed pots by rubbing the surface with a very slightly oily finger. Too much oil will make the surface too shiny and will ruin the effect.*

Above: *This display won a Certificate of Special Merit at the National Exhibition in 1989. The stands are simple, the effort went into the presentation of the trees.*

7 *Glazed pots just need to be washed, but unglazed pots need to be rubbed down with wire wool or fine sandpaper to remove all the blemishes and lime scale.*

Winter protection

Most fully hardy species tolerate having their pots frozen solid for short periods at a time. Pines and spruces even seem to thrive on this treatment, preferring it to any form of protection at all, other than a temporary wind break. But the ravages of winter can take their toll on most other species in a number of ways.

All the effects below can damage a large bonsai but it should survive. Medium-size bonsai – say between ten and eighteen inches tall – can be severely damaged, possibly fatally, while small bonsai are very vulnerable indeed.

1 Good hygiene is essential. Pick off dead leaves, which harbour pests and diseases over winter. At the same time, pick off any scale insects you find.

• Constant freezing and thawing of the pot every day can devastate a root system, especially if the pot never entirely thaws before re-freezing. The root tips absorb moisture but cannot pass it through the frozen roots in the centre of the pot. On re-freezing they expand and burst, just like a water pipe. They can also be crushed by the pressure caused by the expansion of rapidly freezing soil in a container. Remember a waterlogged soil expands more on freezing than a comfortably moist one. Trident maples and Chinese elms have thick, fleshy roots which are particularly at risk. Even large bonsai of these species should be placed in winter confinement.

• Although roots are inactive most of the time during winter moisture is still lost through the bark. Under normal circumstances the tree would contain enough reserves and the roots could replenish the supply during mild weather. Expanding buds also demand a supply of moisture which frozen roots cannot provide. Sunny days can induce both transpiration and bud activity, but may not succeed in thawing the roots as well.

• Cold, drying winds can desiccate fine twigs. Frozen roots cannot replenish the moisture so the twigs die back. Fine-twigged species like birch and Japanese maple are particularly vulnerable, and suffer from the same problem in the wild.

• Wind and sun can cause pots to dry out even in winter. Although this may not affect the tree directly it will kill the finer roots, putting the whole system at risk of decay and more vulnerable to damage by wet, freezing conditions.

• Saturated soil not only increases the risk of frost damage, it also creates the ideal environment for root rot. There is not such a risk if it is raining every day, but if waterlogged soil is left to stand, the risk is increased dramatically.

Protective measures
Having filled you with dismay at the thought of all the dangers your bonsai have to face, let me assure you that by taking a few simple precautions you can guarantee them a long and happy life. Although the worst of the weather comes after Christmas in the northern hemisphere, it is as well to have the protection complete by the end of November. Early damage will only be compounded later. There are five basic ways to site your bonsai over winter, each offering them a different degree of protection.

2 It is a good idea to peel away surface moss, which can harbour insect pests and fungal spores. This is essential on small bonsai which are going to be buried in peat.

Open
Trees are left on benches which are protected from severe wind by a nearby fence or outhouse.

Wind protection
Pots are stood on bricks or boxes between the benches. If the benches run east/west place a board at the eastern end to prevent a wind-tunnel effect.

Shelter
A covered area, closed on three sides and open on the fourth, preferably western side. The

easiest solution is to place the trees on bricks under the benches. Cover the benches with clear polythene and weight it down securely on three sides. In really severe weather the fourth side can be closed off temporarily. Pots should be inspected regularly for dryness. If well constructed, this type of shelter can also double as winter confinement.

Winter confinement

This involves protecting the tree against wind, sun, rain and rapid temperature change. It doesn't offer a totally frost-free environment as this would disturb dormancy in hardy trees. Deciduous trees can be kept in a shed or garage – they need no light until spring. The ideal environment for all trees is a polythene greenhouse, or polytunnel, which can be opened at both ends to allow an air change . To prevent rapid changes in temperature the polytunnel should be shaded from strong sun. Inspect trees regularly for dryness and insect attack.

Frost-free

If you are not sure about the hardiness of an unusual species then it is as well to keep it in a cool conservatory or unheated room through the winter.

What kind of protection?

This depends on the species and the size of the pot. (A three-foot-tall literati in a ten inch pot is a medium sized bonsai as far as climate is concerned). As a rough guide, a tree whose pot is less than eight inches diameter and two inches deep, or the equivalent volume, can be classed as small. Pots up to ten inches in diameter and three inches deep can qualify as medium size. Anything over this is large. The table provides a basic guide. By early spring you can begin to re-introduce your bonsai to their benches, tucking the smaller ones up at night during exceptionally cold weather.

3 Small bonsai should be gently teased from their pots and plunged in a box of loose peat. Cover the root mass with a one-inch layer of loose peat to insulate it.

GUIDE TO WINTER PROTECTION

Large Bonsai
- *Pines and spruces* – open
- *Junipers* – open, give blue-leaved varieties wind protection.
- *Very hardy species (English elm, field maple, larch, birch, hawthorn, yew etc.)* – wind protection. Shelter from prolonged rain.
- *Hardy species (Japanese maples, ornamentals)* – shelter.
- *Temperamental plants (red maples, spring flowering varieties)* – shelter.
- *Trident maples and Chinese elm* – winter confinement.

Medium size bonsai
- *Pines and spruces* – open, wind protection in very severe weather.
- *Junipers, very hardy species* – wind protection, shelter in harsh weather.
- *Hardy species* – shelter.
- *Temperamental plants, tridents and Chinese elms* – winter confinement.

Small bonsai
- *Pines and spruces* – wind protection, very small bonsai need shelter.
- *Junipers, very hardy and hardy species* – winter confinement. Remove smaller trees from their pots and bury them in boxes of damp peat.
- *Temperamental plants, tridents and Chinese elms* – Winter confinement, small trees packed in peat boxes. In extreme cold place trees where the temperature remains just above freezing. An unheated room imay be too warm. A thermostatically-controlled heater for your shed is ideal.

4 An ideal impromptu bonsai shelter. A considerable number of trees can be packed in the spaces below the benches, and the whole thing covered in heavy duty polythene. During spells of really severe weather the front of this shelter is rolled down for extra protection, and the trident maple and Chinese elm are brought into a cold, but frost-free, outhouse.

Pests and diseases

Bonsai are prone to the same diseases and pests that attack full size trees, but because they are small and compact, it doesn't take long at all for a localised problem to spread over the entire tree, with disastrous results. And because it grows slowly a bonsai is less able to outgrow an infection, or a plague of aphids, in the same way a full-size tree can.

A twice-yearly precautionary treatment with a systemic insecticide and fungicide will help, but it will not be one hundred percent successful. (Systemic chemicals are designed to be absorbed by the plant and fight the problem from the inside.) Deciduous trees will benefit from a normal garden 'winter wash'.

Constant vigilance is necessary throughout the year. Once a problem has been spotted and diagnosed remedial action should be taken immediately, using an appropriate commercial treatment.

• Always read the pack to make sure the treatment is effective for your particular problem, and follow the manufacturer's instructions to the letter.

• If one brand doesn't appear to work try another – some insects seem to be able to build up a tolerance if the same brand is used all the time.

• Trees may take weeks to recover from fungal infections, so don't lose heart. If the symptoms stop getting worse, the treatment has more than likely worked.

• Never use systemics on Chinese elms. They will not kill the tree but the foliage will yellow and fall and fine twigs may die back.

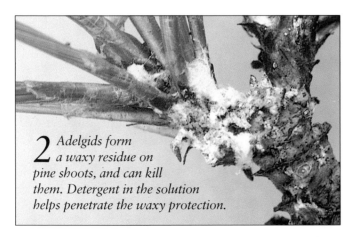

1 Aphids, surely the most common of all pests, here shown in juvenile and adult stage on pine. There are many distinct species, but all succumb readily to conventional garden pesticides.

2 Adelgids form a waxy residue on pine shoots, and can kill them. Detergent in the solution helps penetrate the waxy protection.

3 Scale insects come in many different sizes. These, on a Chinese juniper, are tiny and difficult to spot with the naked eye. Tiny specs of white invite closer inspection.

4 These scale insects are easier to spot once mature. The big ones can be picked off, the smaller ones killed with systemic insecticide. A 'winter-wash' gets rid of overwintering eggs.

5 This ugly little beast is the scourge of all bonsai buffs. It is the notorious vine weevil which can devour a pot full of roots in no time. Treat soil with Gamma HCH and check soil when repotting.

6 The adult vine weevil is not a pest in itself, but it can lay eggs at any time of year. These rapidly hatch, producing the voracious little grub illustrated above. Squash on sight!

7 *These translucent streaks are caused by the leaf miner grub, which burrows its way just below the surface of the leaf. It is unsightly but harmless. Remove affected foliage.*

8 *Papery brown patches like these are most likely caused by too-strong insecticide, or the sun shining through water droplets, which act like magnifying glasses.*

12 *Caterpillars are quite harmless in small numbers. Loners, like this comma butterfly, can be left alone, but remove colonies by hand.*

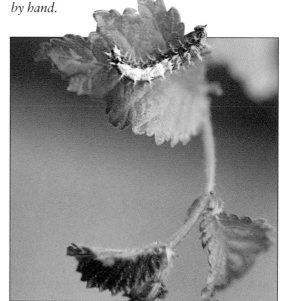

10 *Many trees are attacked by tiny mites which stimulate galls to form on the leaves, like these on elm. Removing all infected leaves in June is the only known cure.*

9 *Red spider mites are microscopic sap-sucking creatures which infest plants in vast numbers, even in mid-winter. The leaves or needles turn brown in patches, and sometimes a minute web can be detected. Cold water spray helps with control, most insecticides are effective.*

11 *'Pine needle cast' starts as yellowing blotches on the needles, which soon fall. This seriously damages full-size trees and can kill bonsai, especially weak or newly collected trees. Once diagnosed, treat monthly with Bordeaux mixture or 'Zineb' until September.*

13 *Poor air circulation is mainly responsible for powdery mildew, which can easily kill young shoots. Cure with appropriate garden fungicide, but prevention is better.*

THE BONSAI YEAR
Month-by-month work schedule

Spring

EARLY SPRING

Excitement mounts as your trees begin to stir. This is the beginning of the busiest season of the year, when you can do a certain amount of creative work as well as more down-to-earth tasks.

Repotting
Any healthy deciduous trees you have not been able to repot yet should be attended to in the first part of this month. If there is no sign of root or bud movement wait a little longer. Continue to keep newly repotted trees away from hard frosts and drying winds. You can keep deciduous trees in an outhouse if necessary at this time. Until the buds open they have no need of light. However, as soon as they begin to burst you must place the tree outside. Don't wire newly repotted trees for three or four weeks, thus avoiding strain on the emerging new roots. Towards the end of the month you can begin to repot junipers and spruces.

Pruning
Deciduous trees can be pruned once the buds begin to show signs of activity. This is so you can ensure that all the remaining branches are alive. Seal all wounds. This is a good time to thin out the fine twigs on deciduous trees so the coming season's growth won't outgrow the design. Remember to prune to a side shoot or to a bud which is pointing in the direction you want new growth.

Wiring
Start wiring deciduous trees – fine twigs as well as thick branches – *before* the buds swell if possible. If the buds have already started to move take extra care as they are easily dislodged at this crucial stage in their development. Trees which have had their fine twigs wired should be kept away from frost and wind until the buds begin to open. Leave three weeks between wiring and repotting.

Watering
Keep soil just moist. Be especially careful not to allow newly-

Because this book will be read in both the north and south hemispheres we refer to the months in this section as parts of a season, rather than by name. The table below gives the equivalent month in both hemispheres.

Northern Hemisphere	Month	Southern Hemisphere
Early spring	March	Early autumn
Mid-spring	April	Mid-autumn
Late spring	May	Late autumn
Early summer	June	Early winter
Mid-summer	July	Mid-winter
Late summer	August	Late winter
Early autumn	September	Early spring
Mid-autumn	October	Mid-spring
Late autumn	November	Late spring
Early winter	December	Early summer
Mid-winter	January	Mid-summer
Late winter	February	Late summer

repotted trees to become too wet. Place them under shelter during rainy spells if necessary.

Feeding
Do not feed newly repotted trees until the buds are open. Trees in training which are not being repotted may benefit from a little bonemeal or fish emulsion.

General
Inspect the soil surface of trees which are not being repotted this year. Remove any dead or disfigured moss and any compacted, 'crusty' soil. Replace it with fresh soil. Check spruces and junipers for red spider mite and aphids and treat if necessary. Both pests can be highly active now, especially on trees which have spent the winter under protection. Sow soft-shelled bought seeds now.

MID-SPRING

Now things are really hotting up. Buds are bursting and roots are growing rapidly. There is so much to do and nature won't wait.

Repotting
If you haven't finished repotting deciduous trees it is best to leave them for next year unless they are really rootbound. Continue repotting junipers and spruce, and begin pines toward the end of the month. Aftercare is the same as early spring.

Pruning
Now you can prune with a little more confidence, since the buds will be opening and you can spot any dead branches or twigs. Seal all wounds. Don't prune spruce or pine now or they will bleed resin, which will disfigure the bark.

Wiring
Wire spruce, juniper and pine but not deciduous trees. Don't wire too tightly because the branches will thicken rapidly for the next month or so. Check small branches wired last month – they may already be set in position!

Watering
Now your watering routine will get under way. During rainy spells shelter newly repotted trees, but you may need to water daily in dry weather.

Feeding
Don't fertilise newly repotted trees. Those repotted last month can be

given their first spring feed if growth has started. A high phosphorus feed is most suitable for these. Use a fertiliser with a higher nitrogen content for trees which have not been repotted.

General

Continue to check for insect attack. Aphids are a particular nuisance because they adopt the colour of the host plant, making them difficult to spot. Clean algae from the trunks and branches. Trees which have not yet shown signs of growth should be placed in a shaded polythene tent. Keep the soil just moist and give a weak phosphorus-based fertiliser.

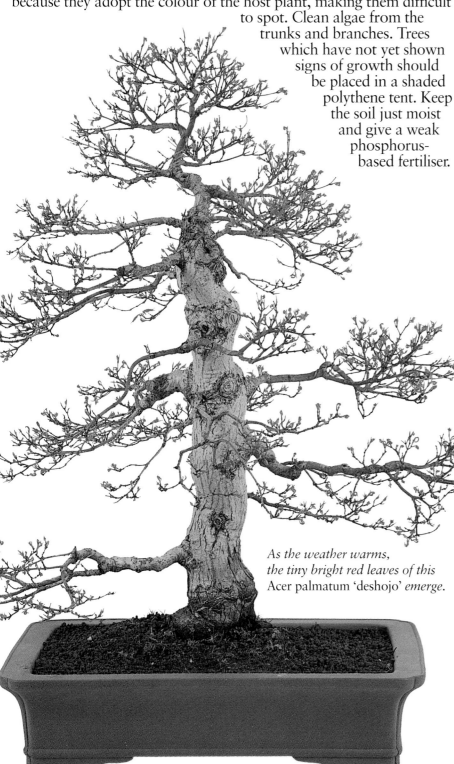

As the weather warms, the tiny bright red leaves of this Acer palmatum 'deshojo' emerge.

Wait until mid-summer before giving up hope. Protect young leaves from hard frosts at night.

LATE SPRING

Pine buds are now beginning to elongate to form 'candles', spruce and larch buds are opening into little tufts of bright green, and all your deciduous trees will now be in full leaf. Spring has happened.

Repotting

All repotting should be finished by the first week. The only exception is Chinese juniper varieties, which can be repotted right through early summer. Only repot other species in emergencies, such as newly-detected root rot.

Pruning

Trees in training can be pruned now but you should already have finished all your deciduous display trees. Still too early to prune pine and spruce. However, dead or dying branches should be removed without delay to prevent any infection spreading to the rest of the tree.

Wiring

Conifers can now be wired, but take care not to damage the new growth. On deciduous trees new shoots may also be teased into position by delicate wiring. If you didn't wire larger branches earlier in the year it is safe to do it now, but new foliage makes access difficult.

Trimming

Pinch expanding pine candles as they grow. Start with the small ones and finish with the larger ones a week or so later. Spruce and juniper may also be ready for their first bout of pinching. New growth on early deciduous trees will need to be trimmed back to two or three buds. Also rub off any unwanted adventitious buds so no energy is wasted.

Watering

Now the trees are in full swing they will need watering at least once a day, but not in full sun if you can help it. Spray the foliage as you go.

Feeding

Late developers can be given a little extra nitrogen, others should now be receiving a balanced diet on a regular basis. Don't feed any trees which have not yet leafed out but spray them daily.

General

All insect pests are highly active now so inspect your trees daily and treat at the first sign of attack. Don't use systemic insecticides or fungicides on Chinese elms. Place sun-sensitive trees such as Japanese maples, azaleas and hornbeams in light shade. There is still a chance of a snap frost until the end of the month – beware! Weeding the pots now will save time later in the year. Be especially meticulous with liverwort and pearlwort – their long roots can quickly clog the drainage holes of the pots. Take softwood cuttings.

Summer

EARLY SUMMER

New foliage is hardening off and flowering is now over. You and your trees settle into a routine which will last for the next three months.

Repotting

Only Chinese junipers can be repotted with confidence now provided they are kept sheltered from drying winds and full sun for a while. Trees which appear too large for their current containers now that they have grown a little can be planted in larger pots provided the roots are not damaged.

Pruning

Start to prune pines and spruce now. Begin with the smaller branches and do the larger ones later in the month. Deciduous trees can also be pruned now but they are likely to throw out vigorous shoots from around the wound.

Trimming

Keep at it. Some trees will have a pause in growth towards the end of the month and a second surge later. This later growth will appear at the tips of the earlier shoots unless they are trimmed back. Keep pinching conifers as they grow. Leaf prune strong trees provided the leaves have hardened.

Wiring

Wire away to your hearts content on anything that takes your fancy. Check wire applied earlier in the year and re-apply if it is too tight. Many deciduous branches will already be set.

Watering

At least once a day. Spray foliage as you water, but not in strong sun as this will scorch the leaves.

Feeding

Continue with a regular balanced feed.

This dramatic little literati style hawthorn was created almost entirely by pruning, from a much larger bush which I rescued from a condemned hedgerow.

General

Continue to inspect for pests and disease and keep pots weed-free. Any trees which show no signs of growth by the end of the month can now be given up as lost. Inspect the plant thoroughly, above and below ground, to try to diagnose the cause of death and thereby learn a lesson. This is a good time to air-layer, pot up new seedlings and begin to take semi-hardwood cuttings.

MID-SUMMER

Your trees will have slowed down by now, resting before their second surge of growth later in the month. Pots heat up and dry out rapidly. Your watering can becomes your constant companion.

HOLIDAY CARE

There are any number of contrivances intended to water your trees for you for two weeks. They include felt wicks trailing from the pot into a bucket, enclosing pot and tree in a polythene bag, and more sophisticated apparatus like automatically-timed sprinklers. None of them are foolproof and there are nearly always some fatalities. If you try any of these the worry will only spoil your holiday.

The best thing to do is give a friendly neighbour (or, better still, a bonsai colleague) the undoubted privilege of caring for your trees while you are away. Ask them to come round a couple of times before you go away, to have a practice run. Many nurseries offer a holiday-care service which is usually quite inexpensive, and is often free.

If neither of these options are possible remove the trees from their pots and plant them in a shady corner, burying the root mass a few inches deep and taking care not to damage the roots. Water the area well before and after planting. The only other alternative is to do what I do: stay home and take your holiday in winter, like your trees.

Pruning

Wounds will heal quickly at this time of year. Good time to prune pines but beware of over-pruning deciduous trees, it is difficult to see the structure through the leaves and you may be making a mistake. This is a good time to create sharis.

Trimming

Carry on as last month where necessary. Junipers will be racing away now and will need a lot of attention. Leaf prune up to the middle of the month.

Wiring

Wire away, especially conifers.

Watering

Carry on as last month, only more so. It is by now especially important to water in the early evening if possible. Leaving large containers of water dotted among your trees can increase local humidity and consequently reduce water transpiration through the leaves.

Feeding.
As last month. Give high potash feeds to flowering bonsai.

General
Continue everyday health checks and inspect wire at the same time. Continue to air layer and pot up seedlings.

LATE SUMMER
Older foliage can begin to look a bit tired this month, although many trees will still be growing rapidly. Next year's leaf and flower are already being set – nature thinking ahead.

Pruning
Wounds heal quickly if pruning is carried out by the middle of the month. Heavy pruning may result in new growth which will not harden off before winter. Carry on creating jins and sharis.

Trimming
This is becoming progressively less necessary now, with the exception of junipers, which will be steaming away for a while yet. Don't leaf prune this month.

Wiring
Wire applied now to deciduous species is unlikely to have much affect until growth starts next year. It is still a good time to wire conifers, especially junipers.

Watering
This is just as hectic as last month. Make sure that pots which become very dry are thoroughly soaked. When the soil has become a little compacted water will often wet the surface and run down the inside of the pot without passing through it. If you suspect this might be happening dunk the pot in the bath for half an hour.

Feeding
Reduce nitrogen this month, eliminating it completely during the last week.

General
Remove weeds, dying leaves and adventitious shoots, and keep up the pest control. Pull any of last year's needles off pine shoots ready for wiring. Take semi-hardwood cuttings and stop air layering by the end of the first week. It is too late to defoliate or to carry out any heavy pruning, as the resulting new growth will not harden off before winter.

In the full flush of summer, this clump-style Japanese maple needs constant attention. Shoots must be pinched almost daily to keep it in trim.

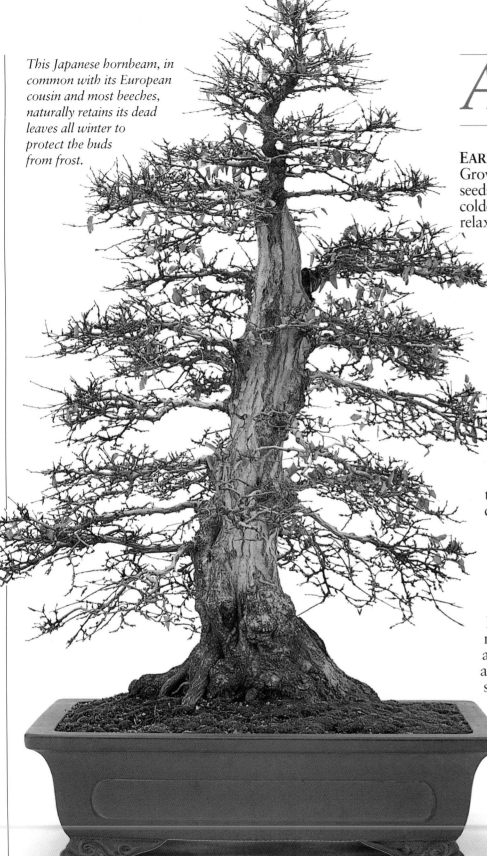

This Japanese hornbeam, in common with its European cousin and most beeches, naturally retains its dead leaves all winter to protect the buds from frost.

Autumn

EARLY AUTUMN
Growth slows to a standstill this month. Roots and buds harden, seeds are dispersed, and inner leaves begin to fall. Sunny days and colder nights induce the first hints of autumn colour. You can begin to relax a little.

Pruning
Only pines, if you must. Deciduous tres may still be boosted into growth, which will not harden in time for winter and will be nipped off by the first frost.

Trimming
Not necessary now – except for those persistent junipers, which will carry on growing for another month or so. Frost will make the newly-pinched shoots turn brown, so be aware.

Wiring
Not advisable. Without new growth the branches are unlikely to set and any fractures in the bark may allow frost to enter over winter, risking damage.

Watering
As your trees begin to slow down so can you. Be vigilant, though, changeable weather can deceive you, and pots can still dry out surprisingly quickly.

Feeding
Nitrogen-free fertiliser all month. Additional bonemeal applied to pines, whose roots remain slightly active all winter, will be appreciated by them early next year.

General
Last chance to do any jins or sharis while the sap is still on the move. Next month the bark will be more stubborn to remove, and the wounds will not begin to heal until spring. Pests are less of a problem now but some are still active on conifers. Sow collected seeds in trays outdoors. Remove debris from both the tree and the surface of the soil to prevent disease. This is a good time to plant new moss. It will continue to grow during mild spells all winter and will have taken hold by next spring. Limit the moss to the area around the roots. A total covering will harbour pests and prevent inspection of the soil.

MID-AUTUMN
'Season of mists and mellow fruitfulness'. Red and gold leaves speckled with dew. Put your feet up and enjoy it.

Wiring
Remove tight wire by carefully cutting it away from the branches.

Don't attempt to re-apply if it involves additional bending of the branch until next spring.

Watering
Only when necessary. For the next two months pots can still dry out but mists and dew may make the surface appear wet, while the soil below may be quite dry. By now you should be able to judge how dry the pot is by the weight.

General
Good hygiene is essential – clean debris from trees and pots. Keep an eye open for plants to dig up for future training. Take hardwood cuttings and sow hard-shelled collected seed outdoors. Start planning your winter protection.

LATE AUTUMN
The last leaves of autumn fall, to reveal the fine tracery twigs your summer-long trimming has produced. Rich, green conifers sparkle with frost. A time to contemplate your bonsai with satisfaction, and appreciate the fruits of your labour.

Repotting
Raw material can be dug up and potted into large containers or growing beds, if the species is fully hardy. Large, fully hardy deciduous bonsai can be repotted now, but only if the roots can be protected from hard frost all winter.

Pruning
Only rough pruning of raw material is necessary. Even well-sealed wounds may die back around the edges over winter if the weather is severe enough. It it advisable to leave short stubs as a precautionary measure. These can be trimmed off next spring.

Wiring
It is tempting to work on your trees when the branches are clear and the structure can be seen. But wiring now will encourage die-back, and lead to disappointment.

Watering
Only when necessary, but check every couple of days. Wind can dry pots almost as quickly as the sun. The greatest danger, though, is over watering, especially in periods of rainy weather.

General
Continue clearing debris, especially dead annual mosses, and any leaves which are caught up in the twigs (leave the dead leaves on beech and hornbeams). These may harbour pests and fungal spores. Prepare your tree's winter quarters by cleaning thoroughly and spraying with insecticide and fungicide. Check every tree for persistent pests such as scale insect, galls etc., and inspect conifers for signs of spider mite. Treat trees with a non-systemic fungicide as a precaution. Take hardwood cuttings, and sow hard-shelled.seeds.

Once this ten-inch tall, formal upright English elm has shed its leaves, the beauty of its fine twigs can be fully appreciated.

Winter

EARLY WINTER
Nature shuts up shop and takes a well-earned rest – but you still have work to do.

Repotting
Finish potting up newly-collected raw material by the middle of the month, and protect the roots from the worst of the weather.

Pruning
Only rough pruning of raw material is safe now. Leave short stubs which can be trimmed off in spring.

Wiring
Tempting, but resist.

Watering
Keep soil moist if the weather doesn't do it for you. Waterlogging can be a problem with trees exposed all winter. Use your discretion, and shelter trees if necessary during prolonged spells of heavy rain.

General
All trees which require winter protection should be accommodated by the middle of the month. Thoroughly clean them first and spray with non-systemic fungicide, if you forgot to do it last month. Photograph your trees as you put them away, as a matter of routine. Hardwood cuttings may still be successful if taken this month.

Clean around your growing and display areas and treat timber with horticultural wood preservative. Spray the surrounding area with insecticide and fungicide to kill off any sneaky pests lurking there.

Make up your Christmas present list of tools, pots, books and other paraphernalia, and distribute it widely!

MID-WINTER
Trees stand motionless, tensed against the cold. The more time you spend with them now, the more you respect their endurance. There is little work for you to do.

Watering
Trees kept in the open will not need watering, in fact they may even need to be protected from excessive rain A thick blanket of snow does no harm to large, hardy trees in the open. But if the thaw is rapid, the trees are likely to receive the equivalent of a week's rain in just one day, so it is wise to clear the snow before this happens. Trees under cover should be inspected weekly and kept just moist.

General
Inspect trees for pests during your weekly water check. Conifers under cover can be devastated by aphids or spider mites at any time during the winter, in a matter of a couple of weeks. Also check the peat boxes you plunged your smaller trees in and clean off any moss.

Give the lower trunks an airing every now and then, during mild spells. Take the opportunity to sort through the photographs of your trees, catalogue your collection and decide which trees to pass on to new owners.

Read books and check stocks of fertilisers and chemicals. Clean pots and equipment and sharpen all your tools.

When repotting time finally arrives there never seems to be enough ready-mixed soil available, so prepare plenty now. Sifting the ingredients will keep you warm.

Hardy bonsai, like hardy trees in the wild, may spend weeks under a blanket of snow, and come to no harm. The snow maintains an even temperature in the pot and prevents transpiration.

Large, hardy conifer plantings, like this Edo spruce group, prefer to be exposed to the rigours of winter. Their green needles, glistening with frost, make a wonderful sight.

LATE WINTER

Deep in the soil something begins to stir. The flower buds on quince and cherries begin to swell. Will this year's spring take a lie-in or will it rise early? A nail-biting time.

Repotting

Truly hardy deciduous trees can be repotted towards the end of the month if the roots are white at the tips. Protect them from hard frost and heavy rain until the buds start to open. Don't feed until spring. Raw material can be dug from the ground and potted into temporary growing containers.

Pruning

You can begin to prune hardy deciduous trees if you are sure the remaining shoots and branches are in good health. Seal wounds and protect from frost until growth has started. Towards the end of the month, last year's shoots and old spurs can be trimmed back to live buds *(see page 56)*.

Wiring

Wire deciduous trees while the buds are still tight against the shoots. As the buds swell they become more fragile and are easily damaged and even more easily dislodged. Don't wait too long or you will get caught out. There is nothing more soul-destroying than spending hours wiring a prize bonsai, only to discover all the next season's potential growth lying on the workbench! Protect newly-wired trees from frost until the buds begin to burst.

Watering

Keep repotted trees moist but not wet. Shelter them from constant rain. Other trees will begin to demand water as they come out of dormancy. It is still very cold and hard frosts will kill roots in waterlogged soil, so beware!

Feeding

Feeding now might damage delicate young roots. Trees which have already started to move, and conifers which did not receive their bonemeal last autumn, can be helped along with a dose of fish emulsion, which is very gentle on the roots.

General

Sudden attacks of aphids or spider mites can defoliate conifers within a week or two, so keep a careful watch. Clean algae from trunks, and remove all scale insects you may find. Take small trees from their peat boxes and return them to their pots. Don't root prune them just yet. Preserve timber benches if you haven't already done so. Plan your workload for the next two months – it will be your busiest period. There is never enough time to do everything, so concentrate on what is necessary at first, and leave what is merely desirable until later. If you do run out of time, these tasks can wait another year.

12 WHERE TO LEARN MORE

Clubs
As you become more engrossed in bonsai there will be occasions when you need first-hand advice. Your local nursery will be able to help diagnose health problems and may even offer a 'hospital' service. But when it comes to solving difficult design challenges or mastering techniques you can't seem to get the hang of, your best bet is to join a bonsai club. Any bonsai nursery will put you in touch with the nearest club. If there isn't one within easy reach you could consider starting one. Again, ask your nurseryman for the address of the national bonsai organisation, who will be glad to help and advise.

At each monthly meeting there is a table show of members' trees, a problem-solving session and a topic for the evening. This can range from a talk on choosing the right pot or a slide show of a famous collection, to a demonstration by a visiting master of an advanced new technique. No matter how experienced you are you will always leave a meeting knowing more.

Workshops
Many clubs and nurseries organise workshops for small numbers of people, where students work on their own material under the guidance of a teacher. These affairs usually last all day and are by far the best way to learn. In many cases it is possible to go along just to watch, but you don't benefit nearly as much as you do by taking part yourself.

Above: This group of English elms was inspired by the hilltop copses of the Berkshire Downs, before they were devastated by Dutch elm disease in the late 'seventies.

Exhibitions
Every year there are several bonsai exhibitions around the country. Studying top-class bonsai at your leisure can be extremely rewarding. You will learn a lot from discovering how others have shaped their trees, and by seeing the results of techniques you have yet to try. Take heart from the fact that many of these specimen bonsai are created from native stock by people who were themselves beginners not long ago.

Above: This maginificent display, modelled on an authentic Japanese bonsai garden, was mounted at the Chelsea Flower Show by members of the British Bonsai Association.

Conventions
Many countries hold annual or bi-annual conventions, which take place over a three-day weekend. These include exhibitions, demonstrations by international masters, workshops and visits to famous collections. There are sales areas offering everything from seeds to specimen bonsai, as well as every accessory imaginable. They attract a large number of enthusiasts from overseas and many firm friendships have been struck at such events.

Every four years a different country hosts the World Convention sponsored by the World Bonsai Friendship Federation, which was inaugurated at the first such event in Omiya, Japan in 1989. This is bonsai heaven, where you can meet top bonsai artists from all over the world who are always happy to pass the benefit of their experience to anyone who cares enough to ask.

You don't have to be an expert to attend an international convention. The only qualification necessary is enthusiasm. And when it's over, and you are on your way home, you will remember when you planted your first seedling in a shallow pot. You will wonder how you could ever have imagined that such a simple act could lead to a whole new world of excitement and challenge, friendship and artistic fulfilment.

Below: The exhibition and sales areas of the International Convention held in Birmingham, England, in 1991. Three days just wasn't long enough to see and do everything.

Above: A colleague of Masahiko Kimura, pioneer of the 'new wave' of bonsai artists, in instructing a nervous English student at the European Convention in Turin, Italy, in 1990.

Below: Enthusiasts from twenty-seven countries gathered to watch the world's greatest masters at work at the World Bonsai convention, held in Omiya, Japan, in 1989.

A silent audience watches respectfully as students work on literati-style bonsai, under the guidance of the Japanese master, Tom Yamamoto.

121

GLOSSARY

This list contains botanical and horticultural terms relevant to bonsai as well as terms unique to bonsai.

ABSCISSION LAYER The layer of cork which forms at the base of the petiole on deciduous trees in autumn. This layer creates a seal preventing the flow of nutrients, causing the leaf to fall.

ACID Describes soils with a pH of less than 7.0. Although most trees will grow happily in acid soils, some, including field maple and beech, do better in alkaline conditions.

ADVENTITIOUS A term applied to shoots arising from parts of the plant other than the growing points, usually on older wood such as trunk or wound scars.

ALKALINE Describes soils with a pH of over 7.0, or rich in lime. Most trees will grow in alkaline soil, but others, notable azaleas, require acid conditions to survive. Alkalinity can be corrected by using any of the commercial soil acidifiers.

ALTERNATE Refers to leaves which appear singly, first on one side of the shoot, and then on the other.

APEX The tip of a shoot, or a tree, from which extension growth takes place. In bonsai this point is dictated by aesthetic considerations and is not necessarily the focus of the tree's energy.

APICAL Describes a shoot at the tip of a branch or a bud at the tip of a shoot.

AXIL, AXILLARY The angle between a leaf and its parent shoot, which always contains at least one bud. Also the angle between a vein and the midrib of a leaf.

BANKAN Bonsai style. A tree with a twisted or coiled trunk.

BARK A protective layer covering trunk and branches , consisting of living corky cells on the inside, generated annually by the cambium, and dead cells on the outside.

BASAL Applies to fresh growth arising from the base of a plant.

BLEEDING The excessive loss of sap from new wounds, often the plant's natural device to prevent infection entering the wound.

BLIND Describes a shoot which has failed to develop an apical bud.

BOLE The clear trunk of a tree, from ground level to the lowest branch.

BROADLEAVED Denotes any tree which is not a conifer.

BUD A tightly condensed embryonic shoot, usually protected by scales formed by modified leaves.

BUNJINGI Bonsai style (Literati). Originating in China during the T'ang dynasty, and reflecting calligraphic brush-strokes.

BUTTRESS The swelling at the base of a trunk where the surface roots emerge.

CALCIFUGE A plant which cannot tolerate alkaline soil.

CALLUS The 'scar' tissue, generated by the cambium, which forms over a wound or at the base of a cutting prior to root initiation.

CAMBIUM The thin growing layer between the bark and the wood which is responsible for laying down new bark on the outside and new wood on the inside each growing season, increasing the girth of the trunk. The cambium layer also forms new roots on cuttings, new buds, and graft unions.

CANOPY The foliage-bearing upper and outer reaches of a tree.

CHLOROPHYLL The green substance in plants, whose function is to convert carbon dioxide from the air, and water from the soil, into carbohydrates, using

sunlight as a catalyst *(photosynthesis)*.

CHOKKAN Bonsai style (Formal upright). A straight, unbroken trunk, persisting to the tree's apex, with symmetrically arranged branches.

COLLAR The swelling at the point of union between a branch and the trunk.

COMPOST 1: Partially decayed vegetable matter. 2: A mixture of

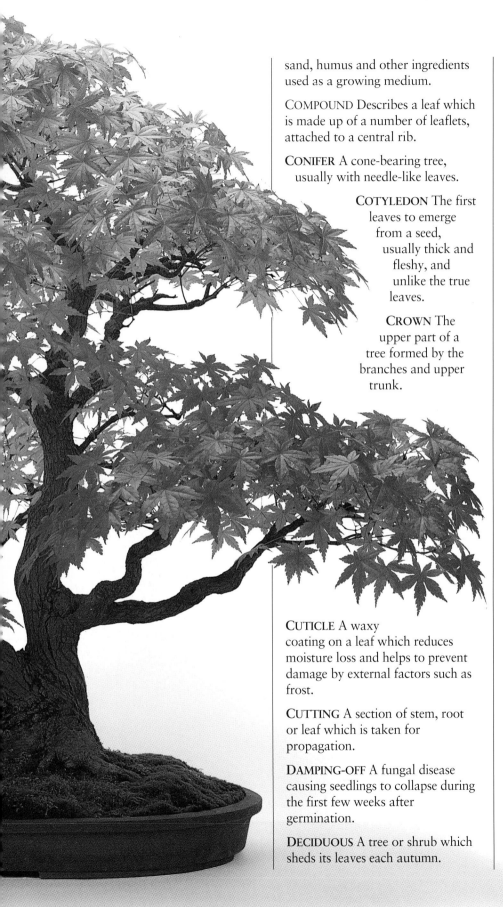

sand, humus and other ingredients used as a growing medium.

COMPOUND Describes a leaf which is made up of a number of leaflets, attached to a central rib.

CONIFER A cone-bearing tree, usually with needle-like leaves.

COTYLEDON The first leaves to emerge from a seed, usually thick and fleshy, and unlike the true leaves.

CROWN The upper part of a tree formed by the branches and upper trunk.

CUTICLE A waxy coating on a leaf which reduces moisture loss and helps to prevent damage by external factors such as frost.

CUTTING A section of stem, root or leaf which is taken for propagation.

DAMPING-OFF A fungal disease causing seedlings to collapse during the first few weeks after germination.

DECIDUOUS A tree or shrub which sheds its leaves each autumn.

DEFOLIATION Natural shedding or artificial removal of leaves.

DENDROLOGY The study of trees.

DIE-BACK The withering and death of shoots or branches due to disease, drought or some other adverse condition.

DORMANT 1: Describes a bud which did not produce growth during the season following its formation, but which retains the ability to produce growth in the future. 2: The resting period during autumn and winter when the tree puts on little or no growth.

DRAWN Refers to plants which have grown uncharacteristically tall and slender due to overcrowding or poor light.

DWARF A genetic mutation of a species producing a small, compact growth habit.

EPICORMIC Refers to growth emerging from dormant buds.

EVERGREEN A tree or shrub which bears foliage throughout the year.

EXOTIC A plant originating from another country, regardless of climate or location.

EYE An undeveloped bud on a shoot over one year old.

FERTILISER A substance which provides one or more essential plant nutrients.

FLUSH A surge of new growth. Most trees produce one flush in spring and another in mid-summer.

FORCING Accelerating the growth or development of a plant by artificially changing its growing conditions.

FUKINAGASHI Bonsai style (Windswept). Depicting a tree exposed to strong prevailing winds.

GALL An abnormal growth on a root, stem or leaf, caused by a microscopic insect.

GENUS A group of related species.

GIRTH The circumference of the trunk of a tree, measured at chest height in full size specimens.

GO-KAN Bonsai style – five trunked.

GRAFTING The vegetative bonding of one part of a plant to another.

HABIT The natural shape or growth pattern of a plant.

HABITAT The conditions and location in which a plant is normally found in nature.

HAN-KENGAI Bonsai style (Semi-cascade). The apex must fall below the rim of the pot but not below its base.

HALF-HARDY Describes a plant which can tolerate cold but not sub-zero temperatures.

HARDENING-OFF The process of gradually introducing a plant grown under protection to outside conditions.

HARDWOOD The term used for timber from broadleaved trees.

HARDY Describes a plant which can survive outside during winter.

HOKIDACHI Bonsai style (Broom). All branches emerge from the same point at the top of a short, straight trunk.

HUMUS Partially decayed organic matter present in the soil.

IKADABUKI Bonsai style (Raft). The plant is laid on its side and the branches are trained vertically to form many trunks.

INORGANIC Applies to any chemical compound which does

not contain carbon. In horticulture the term describes manufactured fertilisers, growing mediums and treatments.

INTERNODE The distance between the leaf nodes on a shoot.

ISHITSUKI Bonsai style (Root on rock) A rock replaces the pot.

JIN A branch or trunk apex which has been stripped of its bark, shaped, bleached and preserved.

JOHN INNES A series of basic compost recipes containing sand, humus, loam and fertiliser.

JUVENILE Refers to foliage produced during stages of rapid growth, which is distinct from adult foliage.

KABUDACHI Bonsai style (Clump). Several trunks arising from the same point on a root.

KENGAI Bonsai style (Cascade). The apex is below the pot's base

KYONAL Proprietary Japanese wound sealant for bonsai.

LATERAL A shoot emerging from a bud on a main stem.

LAYERING A means of propagating from mature growth by removing bark to encourage adventitious root growth to emerge from above the wound.

LEACHING The process by which nutrients and minerals are washed out of the soil by the passage of water.

LEADER The dominant shoot.

LENTICEL A pore on a shoot or stem of a tree.

LIME Calcium as a soil constituent.

LIME SULPHUR Originally used as an insecticide and fungicide, the compound is now used to preserve and bleach jins and sharis.

LOAM Normal, good garden soil.

MAME Miniature bonsai, able to 'sit comfortably in the palm of a hand'.

MOYOGI Bonsai style (Informal upright). The trunk consists of a series of curves with symmetrically arranged branches.

NEAGARI Bonsai style (Exposed root).

NEBARI The exposed surface roots.

NETSUNANARI Bonsai style (Root connected). Several trunks arising from different points on the same root system

NODE A stem joint or the point at which a leaf or leaves are attached to the stem.

OPPOSITE The arrangement of leaves in pairs on either side of the shoot.

ORGANIC Any chemical compound containing carbon. In horticulture the term refers to any compound or growing medium which is not manufactured or synthetic.

PEAT Sphagnum moss or sedge in an arrested state of decay, caused by lack of oxygen in its natural, waterlogged habitat.

PETIOLE The stalk of a leaf.

pH a unit of measuring the acid/alkaline balance of a soil.

PHOTOSYNTHESIS The process by which a plant manufactures sugars by utilising light and chlorophyll to combine carbon dioxide and water.

ROOT HAIRS Single cell projections from the root responsible for absorbing water and nutrients from the soil.

SABAMIKI Bonsai style (Driftwood). The major part of the trunk consists of a shari.

SANKAN Bonsai style (Three trunks).

SAPWOOD The living tissues forming the layers of wood immediately beneath the bark.

SEKIJÔJU Bonsai style (Root over rock).

SHAKAN Bonsai style (Slanting).

SHARI The portion of a trunk which has had the bark removed and has been bleached.

STOMATA The breathing pores on leaves.

SUCKER A new shoot arising from the roots of an established tree.

TAP ROOT The main downward-growing root of a plant or young tree.

TENDER Describes a plant which cannot tolerate low temperatures.

TERMINAL Refers to the upper shoot, flower or bud.

TRANSPIRATION The continual passage of water vapour through pores on leaves and stems.

VEGETATIVE Describes propagation by any means other than by seed.

YOSE-UE Bonsai style (Group or multi-trunked).